WHERE

THE
MONEY
GO?

WHERE DID THE MONEY GO?

Super Easy Accounting Basics for the Business Owner Who Hates Numbers

ELLEN ROHR

www.barebonesbiz.com
877.629.7647
ROGERSVILLE, MISSOURI

For information about this text or the material within, contact the publisher at:
Phone: 1-877-MAXROHR
E-mail: ellen@barebonesbiz.com
            www.barebonesbiz.com

Publisher's Cataloging-in-Publication Data
Rohr, Ellen.
      Where Did the Money Go?: Easy Accounting Basics for the Business Owner Who
      HatesNumbers / Ellen Rohr. — Rogersville, MO: MAXROHR Press, 1999.
            p.   ill.   cm.
      ISBN 0-9665719-2-4
      1. Small business—Accounting. 2. Small business—finance—self-help. I. Title.
HF5657.R64   1999   98-83070
657'.9042   dc—21   CIP

PROJECT COORDINATION BY JENKINS GROUP, INC.

03 02 01 00 ◆ 5 4 3 2 1

Printed in the United States of America

To Frank J. Blau Jr.

My mentor and friend.

Frank, you have done more than anyone

to end business illiteracy

and improve the lives of your fellow business owners.

On behalf of all your 'eagles,'

Thank You.

You are loved and appreciated…and your legacy will go on forever.

Contents

Acknowledgments

"My best friend is the one who brings out the best in me."
— HENRY FORD

To my best friends…

Thank you Dan Holohan. You helped me understand that these words were worth sharing. You are always there with love, advice and support. Thank you so much.

Thank you Al Levi. You always listen thoughtfully to my plans…then insist that I write them down and get after it! Thanks for imposing action and discipline to my grand dreams. This book is a result of your love and help. Thanks, Al.

Thank you Gail Gudell, for de-mystifying accounting with the words, "Ellen, you've got to put it *somewhere*."

Thank you to all my family for love, humor and perspective.

Special thanks to Max and Hot Rod. Thanks for dreaming big dreams with me.

I love you.

Introduction

You own your own business — terrific!

You know how you can be sooooo busy, sales are great, business is booming, and at the end of the month…you haven't made any money!

There is nothing left in the checking account, and there is a stack of unpaid bills on your desk.

WHAT HAPPENED??

This book will teach you the basics you need to keep track of your business… and find out where the money goes! Then you can make sure the money goes where you want it to go…to YOU, your employees and your community.

Some tips for using this book . . .

1. Have your financial statements handy. Read the book from beginning to end to follow the flow of information as Bob Bird's company grows. Look at your financials as you learn the terms and the format.

2. Then use the book as a reference to help you when you dig into your own financial statements.

3. Use it as a training tool to help others at your company understand this stuff, and make the move to Open Book management.

4. If you don't need to know the background accounting, ignore the transaction details in the book. If you are the one responsible for entering data, be sure to figure out the double-entry accounting stuff. That's how you make corrections and adjustments to your financials.

5. This information is available on audiotape! Call me and order toll-free at 1-877-629-7647. It will reinforce your understanding of the information — and it is fun, lively and easy to listen to!

6. Don't expect to become an expert overnight. Like any skill, it takes practice to get good at understanding and using financial information!

7. Learning to understand financial statements is the first step in creating a successful business — lay out the scorecard! That's what this book will do for you!

The next step is figuring how much you should charge for your services! The keys are in the financial statements. The next book in the Bare Bones Biz Basics Series is called *How Much Should I Charge?* This book takes the information from the income statement and helps you create a selling price based on your costs — not some boat-anchor going rate! Call me toll-free at 1.877.629.7647 to order this easy-to-understand guide to making money in your business.

Have fun!

16 REASONS TO READ AND UNDERSTAND *Where Did the Money Go?*

1. So you don't have to pretend you know how to read financials...you'll know!

2. So you don't look stupid in front of your banker.

3. So you can increase your net worth.

4. So you can sleep better at night, knowing where you stand financially.

5. So you can teach your kids, friends, students, employees how to keep score in business so that they can win the game too.

6. Because you love to hear a good story or two.

7. Because you are hell bound on being financially successful and know that the really rich guys know how to read financial statements.

8. Because you want to make a living doing what you love...but you are afraid to lose your shirt in your own business because you really don't know what you are doing.

9. You want to quit your day job and do what you dream of doing...profitably!

10. You want to understand what all those financial words like liability, equity, assets and gross margin really *mean*.

11. You want to sell your company someday.

12. You want to find out if you can afford another truck? Employee? Benefits?

13. You want to be able to determine if you are being ripped off.

14. You want to confront the truth in your business — that it is LOSING money — so that you can turn things around.

15. So you can discover the magic of accountability!

16. Because you want to give generously to yourself, your employees and your community.

My Story...
Why I Wrote this Book.

Once upon a time, my husband "Hot Rod" Rohr and his buddy Richard Yox started a plumbing and heating company called Hot Rod and Yox, Inc. Silly name, but then, they were silly guys. Mostly interested in (winter) skiing and (summer) offering motorcycle rides to unsuspecting young women. I was one such woman, and subsequently became Mrs. "Hot Rod" Rohr. (How could I pass on a name like that?)

Anyway, time marched on and Hot Rod and Yox turned their focus toward the business. Some days, work would get overwhelming. On a Friday afternoon, Yox complained about a remodeling project. He was fed up with the general contractor and our flaky employees. He said, "If I don't do it myself, it will never get done." Yox had worked 60 hours that week, and he wasn't feeling well.

By Saturday, Yox was in the hospital. By Sunday afternoon, he died. He had had health problems for many years, but didn't take great care of himself . . . too much work to do.

We missed Yox . . . his sense of humor and his goofy laugh. He and Hot Rod had been friends since they were eight years old. But, the work, well, it did get done without him. Not just like he would have done it, but pretty darn close. I try to remember Yox whenever I am feeling too almighty important.

Yox had been the bookkeeper at Hot Rod and Yox, Inc. After he died, I raised my hand to take over those duties. Hot Rod had no interest in or affinity for paperwork, and was more productive out in the field. I had a degree in Business Administration, so I figured — piece of cake — I can handle the accounting for a dinky plumbing and heating company. Up until this time, I just ran for parts occasionally, and arranged the weekly golf outing. I was excited to use my store-bought financial knowledge.

Most accounting in small plumbing-heating-cooling companies is done by the plumber's wife. Why? Because she has been formally trained for a PHC financial position? Heck no. Because she watches her husband struggling with the bank statement and finally says, "You go on over to Mrs. Fernwicky's and put in the new water heater. I'll finish this up."

I figured I was a step ahead because of my hoity-toity business education. I was SO WRONG. The next few years were . . . humbling. Every month I would ask, "Where did the money go?"

I didn't know why we weren't making any money. In an effort to cut expenses, I even suggested that we stop generating financial statements more than once a year. After all, we never looked at them. Too depressing!

Then, at Hot Rod's urging, I wrote a letter to Frank Blau. Hot Rod had read an article Frank had written for *Plumbing & Mechanical* magazine about what a contractor should charge. My letter was a request for help — and a pathetic justification of why we were charging $30 per hour.

Frank called me up, told me I had my head so far…Ahem. You get the idea. But he was right. I spent the night burning up the adding machine and discovered what our company was costing per hour to keep it going. In truth, I got sick to my stomach.

But there was no turning back. I had confronted the truth and knowledge imposes responsibility. I called Frank up and asked him if he would help me learn to be a real businessperson. Frank has been my mentor since that day. (Thanks, Frank!)

If I only knew then what I know now!! That financial statements — the Balance Sheet and Income Statement — are the KEY to getting and staying profitable! They are the ticket to sanity in an insane world and the salvation of every struggling business! The SCORECARDS in the game of business!

OK, I'm getting carried away. I'm not the type who LOVES numbers. I'm not neat and tidy, or particularly organized. The only reason I learned about Financial Statements is because our company was sucking the life out of my life. I had to figure out what was going on.

But what I didn't count on was that I would *enjoy* the process…learning to read the reports, watching them improve. **It's fun to keep score!**

In 1995 we sold our company to our employees (the bank was delighted to loan them money based on our financials!), and we bought a 'Gentleman's Farm' in southern Missouri.

Let me help you learn to understand and use Financial Statements. I learned the hard way. I'd love to make it easy for you.

So, that's why I wrote this.

Your Turn...

Why did you buy this book? Go ahead and admit it. Inside, you are really thinking…

▲ "I have never read my financial statements and I have been in business 28 years. Why start now?"

▲ "I HATE numbers. Always have, always will, forever and ever. I bought this book because I should learn this stuff but I will not like this one little bit."

▲ "I have looked at my financial statements. The bottom line anyway. And I'm not making any money. I don't see what this book has to do with making money but I'll give it a try."

▲ "I have no idea what a Balance Sheet is and just a vague understanding of the Income Statement. I know my banker won't loan me any money based on my reports. Maybe it's time I learned this stuff."

Any of these reasons ring a bell?

WHY DID YOU BUY THIS BOOK?

_____

_____

_____

_____

> *"The really rich guys know this stuff."*
> — CHARLES AVOLES

WHAT WOULD YOU LIKE TO GET OUT OF THIS BOOK?

Set a goal:

_____

_____

_____

A Brief Lesson on Goal Setting

Once upon a time, I worked as a ski instructor at the Park City Ski Area in Park City, Utah. (Lousy pay but spectacular work space!) One day my student was a delightful woman named Mildred. Mildred was a brain surgeon! I started the lesson by asking Mildred what she expected out of our day together.

Mildred responded, "I want to be an EXCELLENT skier. I want to be able to ski down any run fearlessly!"

Now, I love a positive attitude. I know that drive and enthusiasm are the stuff miracles are made of. And I am sure that to become a brain surgeon Mildred had accomplished more in the last few years than I would accomplish over the span of several lifetimes. BUT...well, Mildred could barely stand on her skis without tipping over. In fact, she was leaning so heavily on her ski poles that the graphite was in danger of snapping.

As I was a ski instructor and she was a beginning skier, Mildred instantly placed me on the pedestal of highest authority. (I love being placed on a pedestal.) She figured that I had this whole ski thing figured out and could transfer that knowledge directly to her. She was counting on me to make her ski dreams come true.

"Now, Mildred, you may be tempted to do all that IF we have a lot of fun *today*. Because if it's a lot of fun, you might want to go skiing again. You don't have to be an expert to have fun. However, I do believe that the better you get at skiing, the more fun you will have. So let's come up with something fun to do today...like sliding down Bunny Hollow in complete control...without falling down! And you will be well on your way to expert skiing!"

Mildred, naturally, did exactly that. A brain surgeon is butter in the hands of a Professional Ski Instructor.

• • • • • • • • • • • • • • •

So, review your goal...is it something we can accomplish today? Or is today just the kick-off point? Mark Victor Hansen (co-author of *Chicken Soup for the Soul*) suggests that you have TOO MANY goals...wild, outlandish, ridiculous goals. Put down anything you'd like to do. Who am I to say you can't or won't get there or that your goal is unreasonable? And any goal can be broken down into bite-size pieces...

What can we accomplish TODAY?

_____
_____
_____
_____
_____

My hope is that you walk away from this book with…

▲ a better understanding of financial statements and WHY you need the information they provide.

▲ a clear understanding of basic accounting terms.

▲ a commitment to generate and analyze your financial statements by the 10th of the following month — TO THE BEST OF YOUR ABILITY — every month.

▲ usable skills for keeping track of your business and making better management decisions.

…This is what we can accomplish *together.*

If you look at your Financial Statements, analyze them, ask questions, make predictions, make mistakes, fix mistakes…over the course of many months…you will become an expert on your business!

> *"Money doesn't always bring happiness. People with ten million dollars are no happier than people with nine million dollars."*
> —HOBART BROWN

If you want to win at the game of business, you need to keep score.

However…..

If you have more than enough $$$ and your business is making your dreams come true, you don't need this book.

Unless you suspect the future may be different from the present.

I wish this for you:

Make lots of money. Share it. Spend it. Save it. Tithe it.

Have lots of fun and do lots of good with it.

Don't Panic — This Is Only A Test!

So I can best help you become a financial wizard in the span of a few hours, let's find out what you know already. Please take this pre-test. No panicking. If you miss every single answer I won't make you sit in the corner wearing a pointy cap. (Note: There may be more than one correct answer to a question.)

Name:_____

Company:_____

See?! You got the first questions right! Take a deep breath and get set...**Get Ready...Go!!**

1. Another term for Overhead is...
    (✓) Indirect Costs
    (✓) Liabilities
    (✓) Expenses
    ( ) A type of garage door

2. Which of the following items is not found on a Balance Sheet?
    (✓) Inventory
    (✓) Assets
    (✓) Direct Costs
    ( ) Accumulated Depreciation
    (✓) Equity

3. How is the basic accounting formula usually represented?
    ( ) Sales - Direct Costs = Net Profits
    ( ) Assets = Liabilities + Owner's Equity
    ( ) Assets - Expenses = Net Equity
    ( ) All of the above

4. Billable hours refers to ...
    (✓) The direct labor hours for which you bill the customer.
    ( ) The time your bookkeeper spends sending invoices to your customers.
    ( ) The total time your technician is available to do service work.
    ( ) The amount of hours for which you paid your techs, minus the hours actually worked.
    (✓) All of the above.
    ( ) None of the above.

5. It is possible to have a net loss for the month and still have enough cash to run the business for the next two months...true or false?

6. It is possible to have 20% net profit for the year to date and not have enough cash to run the business for one more month...true or false?

7. Below is a list of expense items. Circle the ones that are Direct Costs.

Materials *(circled)*   Tools *(circled)*   Training Seminars
Trucks *(circled)*   Office Supplies *(circled)*   Billable Labor Costs
Permits *(circled)*   Sales commission   Owner's Salary

8. Sales - Direct Costs = _Net_.

9. Another name for Direct Costs is…
   ( )/ Expenses
   (✓) Overhead
   ( ) Cost of Goods Sold
   ( ) Job Site Expenses
   ( ) Those that your boss directed you to expense.

10. What is your deadline to close your books each month? Date_____ and when do you receive the financial statements for the previous month? Date_____

11. *Currently,* when you read your company's financial statements, you …
    ( ) look at trends.
    ( ) look at the past month's activity compared to the year to date numbers.
    ( ) look at budgeted vs. actual amounts.
    ( ) compare this year's activity to the same month in past years.
    ( ) all of the above.
    ( ) none of the above.

12. After you have looked at your company's financial statements, you…
    (✓) file them properly.
    ( ) thank your accountant and pay the bill for his services.
    ( ) call in your managers to explain any discrepancies or questions you have about the information.
    ( ) share the financial information with your employees.
    (✓) think of creative ways to improve performance.
    ( ) all of the above.
    ( ) none of the above.

13. A Chart of Accounts is…
    ( ) the way you code accounting information.
    ( ) the labels under which you file your accounting information.
    ( ) the General Ledger and classifications used in accounting.
    (✓) all of the above.

14. Do you know how much money is necessary, on average, to cover Overhead expenses every month?
    (✓) Yes , $_____   ( ) No, help me!

15. The Income Statement…
    ( ) is another name for the Balance Sheet.
    ( ) summarizes sales revenues and expenses over a period of time.
    ( ) lists the assets, liabilities and owner's equity of your company.
    (✓) all of the above.
    ( ) none of the above.

Good Job! You did it! Now, let's get learning! At the end of the book you can try this test again. You'll be amazed at what you've learned.

Ready? Set. Here We Go!

Coaching Tip: Do you have any financial statements - Balance Sheet or Income Statement - from your company? Pull them out and keep them handy. You will want to refer to them as we learn this information. We'll define terms as we go along.

WHAT THE HECK ARE FINANCIAL STATEMENTS ANYWAY?

A HUGE reason why you may not understand financial information as well as you would like is that the terms are confusing and the words are weird. (Like *vehicular depreciation*.) Also, there are usually several words that mean the same thing. Only, you don't know which ones. So you get lost and confused and feel stupid. Then you give up on the whole darn thing.

Honestly, all we're talking about is keeping score!

FINANCIAL STATEMENTS ARE THE SCORECARD FOR YOUR BUSINESS.

Usually, **Financial Statements refer to the Balance Sheet and the Income Statement.** The Balance Sheet is a report that shows the financial condition of the company. The Income Statement (also called the Profit and Loss statement or the 'P&L') is the profit performance summary. We'll examine the Balance Sheet and Income Statement in detail today. Financial Statements can include the supporting documents like cash flow reports, accounts receivable reports, transaction register, etc. — any report that measures the movement of money in your company. Financial Statements are what the bank wants to see before it loans you money. The IRS insists that you share the score with them, and asks for your Financial Statements every year.

Playing for Keeps

Do you play golf? Tennis? Bridge? Do you ever bet on the outcome of the game? Why? Does it add to the excitement when you "Play for Keeps"? Sure!

My son Max and I play basketball — loser does the dishes. I don't know why I keep agreeing to the bet because I almost always lose! But, it is more fun to have something on the line when we play.

I love Pro Basketball. The Pros play for keeps and I think it makes for very exciting games. I am a HUGE Utah Jazz fan. When they were in the finals against the Bulls, I pitched a tent in front of the TV. Really, I like to watch basketball on TV better than in person. I love hearing the play-by-play and color commentary by the sportscasters.

During the finals, the statistical reports were constant. My heart sank as Karl Malone's dwindling free-throw percentage was plastered on the screen after every trip to the line. It was fascinating to see the stats of each player...who was contributing and who was having an 'off' game. No hiding from the score.

Now, even though Utah had a great team — good attitudes about the game, lots of skills, solid plays — they lost the championship. Could we take the trophy from the Bulls and say, "The Jazz team deserves the trophy. They are such nice guys! Besides, you have lots of these at home?" No ma'am. The Bulls won the game...highest score wins.

Because the Bulls won, does it mean the Jazz are good-for-nothin-losers? Nah. It's just a game. They get to try again next year.

And face it...would the game be as exciting if we didn't keep score? Would you even watch it? Would the athletes even want to play? The statistics take the baloney out of the game. It works or it doesn't. The ball went through the hoop...or it missed. Don't you think the simplicity of sports, the easily identified *truth* of sports, is what makes the games so compelling?

There is an entire industry devoted to keeping track of the Pros. Collectable Basketball cards tell you all kinds of information about what these guys have done...points, assists, free throw percentages. The statistics tell you a lot about a player.

But, not everything.

	Field Goal%	Free Throws%	Rebounds	Assists	Steals	Blocks	Points
Frankie Sharpshooter Guard: 6'1" 180 lbs.							
NBA Career	.494	.856	3.4	9.7	1.4	0.3	17.2
Current Season	.499	.838	3.6	11.4	1.3	0.2	22.5
All Guards	.465	.800	3.0	4.2	1.1	0.2	11.4
Per 48 Minutes	.499	.838	4.6	14.5	1.6	0.2	28.7

What do you know about a player from his stats?

_____

_____

_____

_____

What won't the stats tell you?

_____

_____

_____

_____

FINANCIAL STATEMENTS ARE LIKE THE BACK OF THE BASKETBALL CARD.

A single set of Financial Statements is like one basketball card. You can't tell if you're improving or getting worse. You don't know how you stack up against last month or last year…or the rest of the business world. Your Financials won't indicate whether or not you are a nice person!

However, Financial Statements, especially when analyzed over time, give you incredible information about your company. Primarily, are you winning or losing?? The Financials are the scorecard.

Keep score. Play for keeps. Enjoy the game. Win!

WHAT FINANCIAL STATEMENTS **WILL** AND **WON'T** TELL YOU.

> *"Money, which represents the prose of life, and which is hardly spoken of in parlors without an apology, is, in its effects and laws, as beautiful as roses."*
> —RALPH WALDO EMERSON

Financial Statements will help you…

▲ Pinpoint the strengths and weaknesses of your company.

▲ Create a realistic selling price.

▲ Decide if you should borrow money or borrow more money.

▲ Figure out where the cash goes.

▲ Identify and reward the over-achievers.

▲ Know with certainty your break-even point.

▲ Figure out which jobs are winners and which are losers.

▲ Discover you've got an embezzling problem.

▲ Approach your banker knowing how much he will lend you.

▲ Know what is going on at your company.

The Financial Statements represent everything in terms of money. Money isn't everything but you need a common denominator. Money really does the job nicely. The basic arithmetic used in accounting is addition and subtraction. It really is a nice, neat system of keeping score.

"BUT, MY EMPLOYEES ARE MY GREATEST ASSET."

You might say that your employees are your greatest asset. I would think highly of you if you did. In accounting, people are left off the Balance Sheet. Hard to assign dollar value to — or, worse, claim ownership of — a human being. Still, how you spend money says a lot about how you really feel about your employees. If you love them you will provide training, heap on generous benefits, throw parties for them now and then, and buy Girl Scout cookies from their kids. All those gestures of love are recorded in the Financial Statements. You know the saying…Money Talks!

Financial Statements WON'T tell you…

▲ *How* to get out of a bad financial position. The clues are there but you must make the call.

▲ What lies in the future. Even the most sophisticated forecasting has a solid helping of guess-work.

No, they won't tell you whether a man is good or bad, honest or dishonest…but a man's checkbook will tell you what is important to him.

All in all, the Financial Statements tell you more about your company's performance and financial well-being than any other source of information. By analyzing the Financial Statements every month you will learn to spot trends and discrepancies. A single set of statements is not enough. Like Mildred, you need to get the 'season pass' and put the miles on.

11

How to "HAVE" anything you want in life.

The Financial Statements are wonderful tools...if you are ready and willing to use them to increase your prosperity. BUT...

If you can't accept success and wealth in your life, no amount of financial education will overcome your self-imposed limitations.

You have heard the story...about the fellow who wins $1 million and then loses it a week later. Your wealth is ultimately determined by your ability to have wealth.

A Tale of Champion Level "Havingness"

I have a wonderful friend — Buffy Roper. I met her when we were both coffee shop waitresses in Ocean City, New Jersey.

I hated working there! The manager had the awful habit of referring to himself as 'we' and 'we' never had enough silverware to go around. I used to keep a stash of knives in my apron to make sure my customers didn't have to pick up their chicken fried steak with their fingers! I was just about convinced getting the job was a huge mistake. But, then, Buffy befriended me. She is one of those extraordinary and rare people who is always, every single day, on top of the world. Buffy always had enough steak knives.

Buffy was 19 when I met her. Even then she was absolutely sure that she would...have a fabulous career, marry for love, bear six children, be ridiculously wealthy and travel the world.

Buffy is now 36 years old...and the director of a world class Health-Spa facility, where she often brings a few of her 6 kids (ages 1-8 years old) to work with her. They swim and play while Buffy works out and delegates tasks to her delightful staff. Her husband Rick is a peach, crazy about Buffy and their gaggle of children. He develops land tracts...big ones...when he isn't golfing or collecting antique books or working on independent film projects. Last time I talked to them, they were on their way to the Bahamas...with all the kids. And two nannies. Buffy needed a vacation as she had just completed the New York City Marathon.

So...you can have it all. You must be clear on what you want and address the personal issues that keep you from being successful. Spend time soul-searching...what do you want to be when you grow up? What is your mission, your purpose in this lifetime?

If it were simply a matter of positive mental attitude or affirmations, why, wouldn't it be EASY to be successful? Yes. But, we are more complicated than that. To be sure, our lack of success can be tied to ignorance of sound business practices. But the bigger issue is our lack of self-worth. This book will provide tools and information that can help you create a successful business. IF you will address the personal issues that will sabotage your efforts.

Think you can BE a successful, prosperous businessperson? Good. Then, you must DO what is necessary to HAVE that which you desire. The formula for "Havingness" is

BE → DO → HAVE

Suppose you want to have lots of money...so you can write $1,000,000.00 check to your church's youth group program. First you must BE-come a person capable of wealth. Then you must DO things that ensure wealth...like using financial statements to operate a successful business. Then you can HAVE the rewards.

Here is a partial list of fabulous books to help you increase your "havingness":

Future Diary by Mark Victor Hansen

Your Money or Your Life by Joe Domingues and Vicki Robin

Think and Grow Rich by Napoleon Hill

The Seven Spiritual Laws of Success by Deepak Chopra

Dianetics by L.Ron Hubbard

The Power of Positive Thinking by Norman Vincent Peale

The Great Game of Business by Jack Stack

Dare to Win by Mark Victor Hansen and Jack Canfield

Reclaiming Higher Ground by Lance Secretan

Body and Soul by Anita Roddick

The Business of Contracting by Frank Blau

The Richest Man in Babylon by George S. Clason

The Greatest Salesman in the World by Og Mandino

The E-Myth by Michael Gerber

and sooooooo many more! But these will get you going!

MAKE SURE THAT THE 'BUCKET IS FIT TO FILL WITH WATER.'

Ready to start filling in the scorecard? Let's go! Let's create a make-believe company. As we record the activities of this business we will gain an understanding of Double-Entry accounting and the Financial Statements.

INTRODUCING...EAGLE PLUMBING COMPANY !

"Well, I am not going to snake Mrs. Peabody's drain and that's final!"

Allow me to introduce Bob Bird. Bob Bird has worked for ten years for a plumbing company — Turkey Drain Cleaning. He is fed up with the low pay, dirty work and dead end position he has as the service manager. And he is NOT going to handle the drain cleaning calls just because that good-for-nothing Billy Joe didn't show up today!

Bob wants to strike out on his own. Be the boss. Come in late. Leave whenever. Make the big bucks. He is sick of making other people rich. It's his turn! Bob's Uncle Harry died a few months ago and left Bob $5,000. Bob tucked the $5,000 under his mattress. Let's follow Bob as he starts Eagle Plumbing Company and track every move he makes.

Bob will buy a truck and some inventory. He'll make a couple of sales and pay his bills. For the sake of simplicity, all these activities will occur on a single day: December 31, Year 1.

Extra Credit Question: Can you play out the make-believe financial scenario before you ever started a new company or product line? Before you added the next truck or hired the next employee? Hmmmm?

THE BALANCE SHEET

Let's pull out a blank scorecard: the **Balance Sheet**. The Balance Sheet shows the financial position of the company at a given point in time. Every transaction in the company ultimately affects the Balance Sheet.

The Balance Sheet is like a snapshot of the business. Imagine a newborn baby. That baby's very first picture will record what he looked like on day one of his life. His kindergarten class photo will show you what he looks like at age five. Every photo will capture a specific moment in time. The child's past is still visible in a current photo...the scar on his nose from a bicycle accident. The same features are there, but changed as a result of growth and activity.

So the Balance Sheet reflects the financial condition of the company on a specific date. The Balance Sheet doesn't start over. It is the cumulative score from day one of the business to the time the report is created.

The basic accounting formula is the basis for the Balance Sheet:

$$Assets = Equities$$

LET'S DEFINE A FEW WORDS THAT WILL HELP YOU UNDERSTAND THE BASIC ACCOUNTING 'TOOLS.'

Assets: The 'stuff' the company owns. Anything of value — cash, accounts receivable, trucks, inventory, land. Current assets are those that could be converted into cash easily. (Officially, within a year's time.) The most current of current assets is cash, of course. Fixed assets are those things that you wouldn't want to convert into cash for operating purposes...like your building.

Equities: Funds that have been supplied to the company to get the 'stuff.' Equities show ownership of the assets or claims against the assets.

If someone other than the owner has claims on the assets, it is called a **Liability.**

If you secure a loan to buy assets you would create a liability. Because this is so common, the basic accounting formula is usually presented as:

$$Assets = Liabilities + Equities$$

This is what the whole darn thing comes down to: what you have and how you got it. It is not any more complicated than that.

We will use this basic equation to systematically gather all kinds of information about the company as we record its activities. The activities of a business cause increases and decreases in its assets, liabilities and equities. Accounting uses accounts to, well, *account* for and keep track of those changes. See how simple this is??

Let's keep track of Bob's first business transaction using the Balance Sheet...

Transaction #1

BOB TAKES THE **$5,000.00** FROM UNDER HIS MATTRESS AND OPENS A CHECKING ACCOUNT.

Bob's Uncle Harry was a real character. Chock full of life! Well, until he died, of course. Actually keeled over on the construction site. He was a cabinet maker, still working at 87 years old.

Uncle Harry was very fond of Bob. He used to take Bob with him when he ran for parts. He would philosophize to young Bob. On religion: "If God had wanted man to go to church on Sunday, He wouldn't have invented fishing, football and horse racing." On marriage: "It's a shame that dowry business fell out of fashion." And Uncle Harry's career advice was clear: "Plumbing. Plumbers make all the money. I guess they sock it away in Swiss bank accounts because they don't *look* like they have money. But as sure as my name is Harold T. Bird, plumbing is where the money is!"

So, Bob became a plumber. But his ten years of experience with Turkey Drain Cleaning hadn't left much money in his pocket. When Uncle Harry died, he left a $5,000 inheritance to his favorite nephew. Bob had just shoved the cash under his mattress. Now, he pulled the money out and held it in his hands, the bills spread out like a poker hand.

"Uncle Harry, you're going to be proud of me. Today's the day I start my OWN plumbing business. Thanks for the money and the words of wisdom." Bob raised his eyes to the heavens…and wondered if they had horse racing up there.

So Bob's first act of business as the owner of Eagle Plumbing Company is to set up a checking account with Uncle Harry's $5,000 gift. Let's record this action on the Balance Sheet…

Balance Sheet				
Assets	=	Liabilities	+	Equities
Cash $5,000		Paid in Capital		$5,000

Cash increased. Equity increased. When Bob puts money into his company it's called **Paid in Capital**, an Equity account. It is a reflection of his ownership in the company.

See the how we record the $5,000 twice? This is Double Entry accounting.

MORE DEFINITIONS...

Double-Entry Accounting is a system used to keep track of business activities. Double-Entry maintains the basic Balance Sheet equation: Assets = Liabilities + Equities.

It keeps your accounting system in check.

DOUBLE-ENTRY ACCOUNTING IS BASED ON KHARMIC LAW!

Double-Entry Accounting is based on the basic laws of the universe: what goes around comes around. For every action there is an equal reaction. In one door and out the other. This system of accounting is BRILLIANT and logical and simple. When dollars are recorded in one account they must be accounted for in another account in such a way that the activity is well documented and the accounting equation stays in balance.

Throughout this book we will keep score with Double-Entry accounting. There will be lots of examples to help you understand this accounting method.

The **Chart of Accounts** is the complete listing of all the accounts in the company. It is the *framework* that supports the entire accounting system.

Within the assets, liabilities and equities you can list as many accounts as you need to gather good information about the company and its activities. Your Chart of Accounts can be expanded and adapted to help you gather good data. When you really know what is going on, you have the basis for good management decisions.

The next page has the Chart of Accounts that we will use for keeping track of Bob Bird and Eagle Plumbing. To make the basics easy to follow, I am using a very simple Chart of Accounts. As we go through this book, you will see how we keep score by entering dollar amounts in these accounts. These accounts will maintain the basic accounting equation:

$$Assets = Liabilities + Equity$$

EAGLE PLUMBING COMPANY

CHART OF ACCOUNTS

Account	Current Balance

1-0000	Assets	
	1-1000	Current Assets
		1-1110 Cash
		1-1200 Accounts Receivable
		1-1800 Inventory
	1-2000	Vehicles
		1-2100 Truck - Original Cost
		1-2120 Truck - Accum. Depreciation
2-0000	Liabilities	
	2-1000	Current Liabilities
		2-1100 Accounts Payable
	2-2000	Long Term Liabilities
		2-2100 Note Payable - Truck Loan
3-0000	Equity	
	3-1000	Paid-In Capital
	3-8000	Retained Earnings
	3-9000	Current Year Endings
4-0000	Income	
	4-1000	Sales
5-0000	Direct Costs	
	5-1000	Materials
	5-2000	Billable Labor
	5-3000	Permits
6-0000	Indirect Costs	
	6-1000	Owner's Salary
	6-1050	Non-Billable Labor
	6-2000	Advertising
	6-2050	Depreciation
	6-3000	Education
	6-3050	Insurance
	6-3075	Miscellaneous
	6-4000	Office Supplies
	6-4050	Professional Services
	6-4075	Shop Supplies
	6-5000	Tools
	6-5050	Truck Maintenance & Repair
	6-6000	Uniforms
8-0000	Other Income	
9-0000	Other Expenses	
	9-1000	Taxes

MORE DEFINITIONS...

The activity for each account can be illustrated in an **account.** You use **debits** and **credit** increase or decrease the accounts depending on the type of transaction.

Here is how transaction #1 is recorded in the Cash account and the Paid in Capital account.

Cash	
Debit	Credit
$5000 (#1)	

Paid in Capital	
Debit	Credit
	$5000 (#1)

Each account is cumulative and shows all the transactions that affect that account. To keep all the transactions straight in our examples, I will put the transaction number next to each item.

Once upon a time when all accounting was manual, these were referred to as 'T'-accounts. (Because they are set up like a 'T'. See it?) Makes sense, huh?

You see, the 'T' helps keep the debit-credit thing straight. I won't fuss too much over the mechanics of the debits and credits. There is a handy debit and credit rules reference guide in the very back of the book. For now, just try to follow the illustration.

The **General Ledger** contains the information collectively for each account. Picture the General Ledger as a big book where all the accounts are listed. (In a computerized accounting program you can run a **Detail Trial Balance** report to print the information in the General Ledger.)

Note: Check with your accountant and your own software manuals to find out what the reports are called for your accounting system. I've tried to use the most common terms but the words can vary from program to program.

The **Journal** is a record of all the transactions in the order in which they occur. The Journal Entries are then posted to the General Ledger. The Journal can also be called the **Transaction Register.** Think of the Journal as the diary, the day-by-day record of what happened in the company.

THE ACCOUNTS, THE JOURNAL AND THE GENERAL LEDGER CONTAIN THE BACKGROUND INFORMATION FOR THE FINANCIAL STATEMENTS.

This is where you look to find the details, or to uncover a mistake.

You probably will use some kind of accounting software to help you keep score. Here's what the Journal (Transaction Register) would look like for transaction #1:

EAGLE PLUMBING COMPANY
JOURNAL
12/31/YEAR 1

Date	Account #	Debit	Credit
12/31/Year 1	#1 - Bob takes money from under his mattress.		
	1-1110 Cash	$5,000.00	
	3-1000		$5,000.00
	Grand Total:	$5,000.00	$5,000.00

Here's what the General Ledger (Detail Trial Balance) would look like for transaction #1:

EAGLE PLUMBING COMPANY
GENERAL LEDGER
DETAIL TRIAL BALANCE
12/31/YEAR 1

Date	Memo	Debit	Credit	Net Activity	Ending Balance
1-1110 Cash			Beginning Balance:	$0.00	
12/31/Year 1 #1 - Bob takes money from		$5,000.00			$5,000.00
	Total:	$5,000.00	$0.00	$5,000.00	$5,000.00
3-1000 Paid in Capital			Beginning Balance:	$0.00	
12/31/Year 1 #1 - Bob takes money from			$5,000.00		$5,000.00 cr
	Total:	$0.00	$5,000.00	$5,000.00 cr	$5,000.00 cr
	Grand Total:	$5,000.00	$5,000.00		

Whew! Lots of definitions and concepts! Time for some more examples to help your understanding…

Let's look at Bob's next move and see the effect on the Balance Sheet and the supporting evidence in the Accounts, the Journal and the General Ledger.

> *With money in your pocket, you are wise and you are*
> *handsome and you sing well too.*
> —YIDDISH PROVERB

Transaction #2

BOB BUYS A TRUCK.

Bob is feeling pretty flush with that $5,000 in the bank. Time to spend some money! To get his plumbing business off the ground, Bob needs a truck. Bob is in absolute heaven. He just loves trucks and today he's going to buy one! The only new truck he has ever had was the one he bought when he was sixteen years old. He recalls every detail of that rig. It was a Jeep Wrangler. Painted all red, white and blue…kind of a stars and stripes theme. The stinky-new smell of the vinyl seats 'outgassing.' The tires that were still so new they hadn't worn off the little rubber, mold-injected-excess bits. The first day he owned it he took the motor out of that brand new vehicle, oiled everything and put it back in. Just because he could. He loved it so much. Actually named it 'Stevie,' after Stevie Nicks of Fleetwood Mac.

Alas, now, he only has $5,000 in the checking account. Trucks nowadays cost ten times what they did when he was in high school. Even if he forgoes the sweet Ford 4x4 'dually' with the pin stripes and the air brushed "Dogs Playing Poker" artwork, Bob will need to borrow some money. Settling down a little, Bob selects a very functional one-ton van with utility shelving. The salesman, eager to cut a deal, agrees to loan Bob the full $15,000 to purchase the truck. Let's record the transaction…

	Balance Sheet			
Assets	=	Liabilities	+	Equities
Cash $5,000			Paid in Capital	$5,000
Truck $15,000		Loan	$15,000	
Totals = $20,000	=		$15,000 +	$5,000

So, the basic equation stays in balance. I bet you understand why it's called the Balance Sheet by now, huh? Look back at page 16. Note the changes for each account. The Balance Sheet shows the *cumulative* effect of Bob's business activities.

Check out the accounts and the Journal Entries. This is the detail behind the information on the Balance Sheet. Notice that each account shows the total of the account. The accounts show all the details of the activities.

Accounts

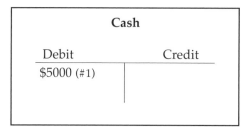

Cash	
Debit	Credit
$5000 (#1)	

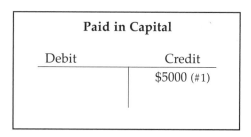

Paid in Capital	
Debit	Credit
	$5000 (#1)

Cash	
Debit	Credit
$15000 (#2)	

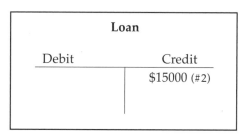

Loan	
Debit	Credit
	$15000 (#2)

Note: Total Debits always equal total Credits. It's a function of the Balance Sheet Formula:

- Asset = Liabilities + Equity.
- Assets have a Balance in the Debit Column.
- Liabilities and Equity have a balance in the Credit Column.

If you want to get into detail, check the last page of this book for a reference guide for Debit and Credit rules.

EAGLE PLUMBING COMPANY

JOURNAL

12/31/YEAR 1

Date	Account #	Account Name	Debit	Credit
12/31/Year 1	#1 - Bob takes money from under his mattress.			
	1-1110	Cash	$5,000.00	
	3-1000	Paid- in Capital		$5,000.00
12/31/Year 1	#2 - Bob buys a truck.			
	1-2100	Truck - Original Cost	$15,000.00	
	2-2100	Note Payable - Truck Loan		$15,000.00
		Grand Total:	$20,000.00	$20,000.00

EAGLE PLUMBING COMPANY
GENERAL LEDGER
DETAIL TRIAL BALANCE

12/31/YEAR 1

Date	Memo	Debit	Credit	Net Activity	Ending Balance
1-1110 Cash			Beginning Balance:	$0.00	
12/31/Year 1 #1 - Bob takes money from		$5,000.00			$5,000.00
	Total:	$5,000.00	$0.00	$5,000.00	$5,000.00
1-2100 Truck - Original Cost			Beginning Balance:	$0.00	
12/31/Year 1 #2 - Bob buys a truck.		$15,000.00			$15,000.00
	Total:	$15,000.00	$0.00	$15,000.00	$15,000.00
2-2100 Note Payable - Truck Loan			Beginning Balance:	$0.00	
12/31/Year 1 #2 - Bob buys a truck.			$15,000.00		$15,000.00 cr
	Total:	$0.00	$15,000.00	$15,000.00 cr	$15,000.00 cr
3-1000 Paid-in Capital			Beginning Balance:	$0.00	
12/31/Year 1 #1 - Bob takes money from			$5,000.00		$5,000.00 cr
	Total:	$0.00	$5,000.00	$5,000.00 cr	$5,000.00 cr
	Grand Total:	$20,0000	$20,000.00		

You might be more familiar with a Balance Sheet that is formatted like this:

EAGLE PLUMBING COMPANY

BALANCE SHEET

DECEMBER 31, YEAR 1

Assets			
Current Assets			
Cash	$5,000.00		
Total Current Assets		$5,000.00	
Vehicles			
Truck - Original Cost	$15,000.00		
Total Vehicles		$15,000.00	
Total Assets			$20,000.00
Liabilities			
Long Term Liabilities			
Note Payable - Truck Loan	$15,000.00		
Total Long Term Liabilities		$15,000.00	
Total Liabilities			$15,000.00
Equity			
Paid-in Capital		$5,000.00	
Total Equity			$5,000.00
Total Liability & Equity			$20,000.00

Still in balance, still holds to the basic equation…Assets = Liabilities + Equity. Note that the dollar amount is increasing. The company is growing.

At this point the company is growing as a result of 'Other People's Money' flowing into the company via the Ford loan. One way to get cash is to put money directly into the checking account. If the owner supplies the cash, it is recorded as Paid-In Capital. The owner thereby increases his equity, ownership, in the company. If someone else supplies the cash, by way of a loan, a liability is created.

When a new company starts up, it will need some cash to get going. Ultimately the cash needed to run the company should come from selling goods and services! But hang on…we'll address that in a few pages!

MORE ABOUT ASSETS & LIABILITIES ...

Not all assets are the same! Cash is king! Cash is so useful! On the other hand, your truck, though also an asset, is not as flexible. You don't want to sell your truck and use the cash to pay the phone bill. Make sense? So, we categorize the assets — cash, and other assets that could be converted to cash within a year's time, are called Current Assets.

CURRENT ASSETS INCLUDE:

- ▲ **Cash**...the green stuff and coins! Money in the bank.
- ▲ **Accounts Receivable**...when you do the work today and someone promises that they will pay you for the work next month, that promise is called an account receivable. It's a current asset because by next month — you hope — it will be paid, and turn into cash in the bank.
- ▲ **Inventory**...when you buy inventory the idea is to sell it (and the labor to install it) and create cash, or accounts receivable.
- ▲ Assets that are not as easily converted to cash — or shouldn't be sold just to create cash — are called **Fixed Assets**. These include vehicles, tools, buildings and land. These assets are best used for operating the business and doing the work — not for selling in order to create cash to pay bills.

Liabilities are also broken down into two basic categories...Current Liabilities are short term liabilities, obligations that are due within the next twelve months. Long term liabilities are obligations that give you more than a year to pay them back. Make sense?

CURRENT LIABILITIES INCLUDE...

- ▲ **Accounts Payable**...when you buy something from somebody — like materials for a job — you may promise to pay them in 30 days. That promise is called an account payable.
- ▲ **Sales tax and payroll taxes** may also be accounted for as payables.

So, it's important to watch the amounts in the current assets and current liabilities. You need more in current assets than current liabilities or you will be unable to pay your bills! This measurement of current assets to current liabilities is called your **current ratio**.

CURRENT ASSETS : CURRENT LIABILITIES

You will sleep better at night if you can maintain a 2:1 current ratio! In other words, aim for twice as much in current assets as you owe in current liabilities. If you want your bank to loan you money, they will look at your current ratio to determine your ability to pay your bills on time.

How are you doing? Try to follow the flow of the money and the impact of the transactions on the reports. It's not so hard is it?

Transaction #3

BOB GOES SHOPPING.

Bob spends the day driving around in his new truck. He is so pleased with himself. He is following his dream…he's an independent business owner, an entrepreneur!

He swings the truck into the supply house yard. Bob saunters to the counter. These guys know him. He has picked up parts from this wholesaler for the last ten years. Oh, the hours he has spent here, whining about his *former* boss, "If I ran the show, things would be different. How can I get any work done when I am always here, waiting on my parts order ?? My boss never stocks what we need! When I go out on my own I will load up on the inventory."

Of course, Bob doesn't have an account set up yet, so today he pays cash for his purchases. He buys $3,000 worth of ballcocks, nipples and male and female adapters to keep on his truck. (No doubt, plumbing repair parts have the oddest names!) Feeling like a man who has set the world straight, Bob saddles up in his new truck and heads off into the sunset…and off to make his first sale!

Let's track Bob's purchases on the Balance Sheet. Cash decreases. Inventory appears on the Balance Sheet. He swapped one asset for another one.

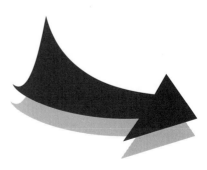

EAGLE PLUMBING COMPANY

BALANCE SHEET

DECEMBER 31, YEAR 1

Assets
  Current Assets
    Cash $2,000.00
    Inventory $3,000.00
  Total Current Assets $5,000.00
  Vehicles
    Truck - Original Cost $15,000.00
  Total Vehicles $15,000.00
Total Assets $20,000.00

Liabilities
  Long Term Liabilities
    Note Payable - Truck Loan $15,000.00
  Total Long Term Liabilities $15,000.00
Total Liabilities $15,000.00

Equity
  Paid-in Capital $5,000.00
Total Equity $5,000.00

Total Liability & Equity $20,000.00

HELPFUL HINTS

Compare the Balance Sheet with the one on page 25. While the total numbers stay the same, you can see that Bob is in a different cash position now. With each transaction, flip back to the previous transaction and compare the reports. What changed? This will help you understand this stuff!

Look at the accounts after transaction #3.

Cash	
$5000 (#1)	$3000 (#3)
Bal: $2000	

Paid in Capital	
	$5000 (#1)

Truck	
$15000 (#2)	

Loan	
	$15000 (#2)

Inventory	
$3000 (#3)	

Look at the Journal and General Ledger for transaction #3.

EAGLE PLUMBING COMPANY
JOURNAL

12/31/YEAR 1

Date	Account #	Account Name	Debit	Credit
12/31/Year 1	#1 - Bob takes money from under his mattress.			
	1-1110	Cash	$5,000.00	
	3-1000	Paid-in Capital		$5,000.00
12/31/Year 1	#2 - Bob buys a truck.			
	1-2100	Truck - Original Cost	$15,000.00	
	2-2100	Note Payable - Truck Loan		$15,000.00
12/31/Year 1	#3 - Bob goes shopping.			
	1-1800	Inventory	$3,000.00	
	1-1110	Cash		$3,000.00
		Grand Total:	$23,000.00	$23,000.00

EAGLE PLUMBING COMPANY
GENERAL LEDGER
DETAIL TRIAL BALANCE

12/31/YEAR 1

Date	Memo	Debit	Credit	Net Activity	Ending Balance
1-1110 Cash			Beginning Balance:	$0.00	
12/31/Year 1 #1 - Bob takes money from		$5,000.00			$5,000.00
12/31/Year 1 #3 - Bob goes shopping.			$3,000.00		$2,000.00
	Total:	$5,000.00	$3,000.00	$2,000.00	$2,000.00
1-1800 Inventory			Beginning Balance:	$0.00	
12/31/Year 1 #3 - Bob goes shopping.		$3,000.00			$3,000.00
	Total:	$3,000.00	$0.00	$3,000.00	$3,000.00
1-2100 Truck - Original Cost			Beginning Balance:	$0.00	
12/31/Year 1 #2 - Bob buys a truck.		$15,000.00			$15,000.00
	Total:	$15,000.00	$0.00	$15,000.00	$15,000.00
2-2100 Note Payable - Truck Loan			Beginning Balance:	$0.00	
12/31/Year 1 #2 - Bob buys a truck.			$15,000.00		$15,000.00 cr
	Total:	$0.00	$15,000.00	$15,000.00 cr	$15,000.00 cr
3-1000 Paid-in Capital			Beginning Balance:	$0.00	
12/31/Year 1 #1 - Bob takes money from			$5,000.00		$5,000.00 cr
	Total:	$0.00	$5,000.00	$5,000.00 cr	$5,000.00 cr
	Grand Total:	$23,000.00	$23,000.00		

Right about now you may be asking yourself...

If my accounting system is computerized, do I need to know this stuff?

The Answer: No and Yes.

You DON'T need to know the fine points of bookkeeping and accounting. Your accountant needs to know them and your bookkeeper needs to know them. Your computerized accounting system will probably handle all the double-entry stuff just fine.

I NEVER wanted to learn the numbers. I am much too flighty and my attention span is much too short for all this hard facts stuff. But I had to learn this because our business was ruining my life. Once I got into it, I found out how fun it is to keep score.

I also found out all the mistakes that my accountant had been making! It wasn't her fault. I had given her vague information and had never checked the reports!

You need to know how to read, interpret and act on the Financial Statements. Your assessment of the Financials will be enhanced if you know what they are and how they account for different activities. A basic understanding of how a tool works will help you use that tool better.

It may be that you are the bookkeeper and accountant for your company. If so, this overview of Double-Entry accounting will help you see the framework on which all your data entry hangs. This will make it easier to correct erroneous information. Could it be that you have some reports that you don't trust? Do you want to change your accounting to generate better managerial data? An understanding of Double-Entry accounting will help you fine tune your information.

You need to know that the information you get from your Financials is correct. I would lay $1,000 down that you will find major information that is just plain WRONG in your Financials once you start checking them out on a regular basis. Common problem? Garbage in, garbage out. Unless the data entry person knows where the data is supposed to be entered, your information will be worthless.

You don't need to know everything about accounting. **You do need to know everything in this book...as a bare minimum!**

Let's use what we know from the Financials and do some analysis...

Bob's inventory purchase affected his **cash flow**. Although the total value of the assets didn't change on the Balance Sheet, Bob has to pay special attention to cash. It works better for buying things than swapping with chickens. Of all assets, cash is the most precious.

Play with a couple of "What If?" transactions and see how they would affect Bob's business.

What if...
▲ Bob wanted to borrow $1 million for a new building. Could he?
▲ Bob's buddy Phil wanted to invest $40,000 into the company. Beware!
▲ Bob can get a great deal on low-flush toilets! If he buys 100 of them, he only pays $50 each. Is that a good deal?
▲ If Bob fills his propane tanks in July, he only pays $.65 per gallon, as opposed to $1.39 per gallon he expects to pay in December. Should he stock up?

What are the Cash Flow implications of each of these activities?

Cash Flow: The movement and timing of money, in and out of the company. The heartbeat of a business is Cash Flow.

A **cash flow statement** is a report that shows, month by month, how much money you predict will come into and flow out of your company. Bankers love this. You can use it for a budget.

Could you have lots of cash on hand and still be losing money in your business?? YES! Could you be profitable...but your checking account is empty? YES!

Do you use **Cash Basis** or **Accrual Basis** accounting at your company?

Cash Basis Accounting: When you account for your business activities, no adjustments are made for pre-paid expenses or unearned income. You record the transaction in full on the day the money shows up, or leaves the company.

Accrual Basis Accounting: When you account for your business activities, you adjust for pre-paid and unearned items. Under this basis, revenues (Sales) are credited to the time period in which they are earned, and expenses are credited to the time period in which they are incurred.

Whew...lots of mumbo jumbo. Let's use an example to clarify.

Let's say Bob Bird needs propane to heat his shop. To take advantage of the summer selling price of the fuel, he buys a year's supply of propane in July. He writes a check for $2,000.

With Cash Basis Accounting, Bob would expense the entire amount in the month the check was written — July. With Accrual Basis Accounting, Bob would determine how much fuel would be used each month, and expense that amount each month. By either exact fuel monitoring or a well thought out guess, Bob can account for a portion of the fuel expense each month.

However, for managerial reasons, your internal information should always be calculated on an Accrual Basis.

Accrual basis accounting is more accurate. It shows a truer picture of what is happening at your company. You can also create a cash flow statement (report) to keep an eye on cash available and cash needed from day to day, week to week.

HERE'S A BONUS ROUND QUESTION:
WHAT IS BOB'S NET EQUITY IN HIS COMPANY?

Net Equity = Total Assets - Total Liabilities

So at this point Bob's Net Equity is $5,000 ($20,000 - $15,000). **Net Equity is also called Net Worth** and it reflects Bob's ownership of the Assets. Notice that we are just restating the basic accounting formula: Assets = Liabilities + Equity.

Be aware that Net Worth is not what the company is worth. Would you like to sell your company some day? Great. Be aware that the selling price of your company will be based on its ability to *generate money*, not on Net Worth or Assets. Profit! Ah, that is the breath of life for your company. Let's check in with Bob Bird and see if he can generate some profit dollars with his company.

HELPFUL HINTS

You can set up a Balance Sheet for yourself and your family — and I suggest you do! It's great to see what you HAVE (assets) and take note of what you OWE (liabilities) and realize the difference (net worth) ... what you OWN. Unlike a business, personal net worth is a good measure of your family fortune. Do you aspire to a debt-free life? Do you want to build your investments and real estate holdings? You can keep score with a personal Balance Sheet and Income Statement.

> *"I am indeed rich, since my income is superior to my expense, and my expense is equal to my wishes."*
> EDWARD GIBBONS

THE INCOME STATEMENT

Bob Bird is ready to plumb! Let the phone ring; let the sales begin! How do we account for Sales?

Let's pull out another scorecard: The Income Statement. The **Income Statement** (also called a **Profit and Loss Statement** or a 'P&L') is a report that shows changes in the Equity of the company. Expenses are decreases in Equity. Revenues are increases in Equity. The basic equation for the Income Statement is

$$Revenues - Expenses = Profit$$

If the Expenses are greater than the Revenues we get a negative profit. Also known as a — *gulp* — Loss.

The Income generated during the month gets transferred to the Balance Sheet at the end of the month. In fact, the Income Statement is like a magnifying lens on the activities that effect the changes in the Equity of the company. The profits from the month increase the Equity of the company. A Loss results in a decrease in Equity.

MORE DEFINITIONS....

The Income Statement and the Balance Sheet are connected. The Net Profit dollar amount of the Income Statement is the **Current Earnings** dollar amount on the Balance Sheet. You see, the net change in the Equity section of the Balance Sheet is Net Profit.

The cumulative account for all the earnings for the company is called **Retained Earnings**. At the end of the year, the Current Earnings number moves down to the Retained Earnings spot in the Equity Section. Why? Well, they aren't current any more!

While the Balance Sheet gives you a snapshot of the company's financial well being, the Income Statement shows you revenues and expenses over a period of time. Usually over a month or a year, although you could generate Income Statements every day.

Understanding and analyzing your Income Statements can help you with these decisions…
▲ How much do I need in Sales to achieve my goals?
▲ Is my selling price adequate?
▲ Am I spending too much or too little on _____?

The Income Statement answers the question WHERE DID THE MONEY GO???

The Income Statement tells you **how much money you made OR LOST during the accounting period**.

So, let's follow Bob Bird on his first sale…

The income statement is like a magnifying glass on the activities that impact the ups and downs in the equity of your company.

Transaction #4

BOB SELLS A HOSEBIB.

The phone rings! "Thank you for calling Eagle Plumbing, how may I help you?" Bob answers in his most professional voice.

"Yo Bob, this is Fred, from next door. Do you have one of those things that you turn off the water to the hose with?" asks Fred Freeload, Bob's next door neighbor.

"You mean a silcock?" Bob responds.

"A what? No, man, I mean a thingy that shuts the water off to the hose. Mine's busted."

Bob is used to Fred calling and 'borrowing' things like replacement toilet parts and water heater elements. Things that usually get installed, not returned. Fred fancies himself a do-it-yourself-er. But Fred's mechanical skills are limited…and his DIY jobs usually turn into day long projects for Bob once he comes to the rescue. Bob sighs and decides to charge Fred for the part…with something extra for the time Bob is sure to spend helping out. Bob paid $95 for the silcock (a.k.a. a hosebib) at the supply house and, pulling a selling price out of thin air, he sells it to Fred for $150.

Here's how we record the transaction on a simple Income Statement. The Expense in this transaction is the hosebib.

EAGLE PLUMBING COMPANY
INCOME STATEMENT

12/31/YEAR 1

Income		
Sales	$150.00	
Total Income		$150.00
Direct Costs		
Materials	$95.00	
Total Direct Costs		$95.00
Gross Profit		$55.00
Net Profit/(Loss)		$55.00

Here's how transaction #4 affects the Balance Sheet:

EAGLE PLUMBING COMPANY
BALANCE SHEET

DECEMBER YEAR 1

Assets			
Current Assets			
Cash	$2,150.00		
Inventory	$2,905.00		
Total Current Assets		$5,055.00	
Vehicles			
Truck - Original Cost	$15,000.00		
Total Vehicles		$15,000.00	
Total Assets			$20,055.00
Liabilities			
Long Term Liabilities			
Note Payable - Truck Loan	$15,000.00		
Total Long Term Liabilities		$15,000.00	
Total Liabilities			$15,000.00
Equity			
Paid-in Capital		$5,000.00	
Current Year Earnings		$55.00	
Total Equity			$5,055.00
Total Liability & Equity			$20,055.00

Compare this to the Balance Sheet on Page 28. Note the changes.

This transaction affects a few accounts.
- ▲ There is an increase in Cash of $150.
- ▲ The hosebib leaves Inventory...decrease of $95.
- ▲ The profits from the Income Statement transfer to the Balance Sheet as an increase in Equity, recorded as Current Earnings.

The Balance Sheet shows that Eagle Plumbing is growing again. **This time Income from operating the business increases Bob's Equity. Cool, huh?!**

Here are the Accounts

Cash	
$5000 (#1)	$3000 (#3)
$150 (#4)	
Bal: $2150	

Loan	
	$15000 (#2)

Truck	
$15000 (#2)	

Paid In Capital	
	$5000 (#1)

Inventory	
$3000 (#3)	$95 (#4)
Bal: $2905	

Sales	
	$150

Is it becoming clear?

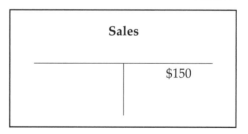

Direct Costs	
$95 (#4)	

Eagle Plumbing Company
Journal

12/31/Year 1

Date	Account #	Account Name	Debit	Credit
12/31/Year 1	#1 - Bob takes money from under his mattress.			
	1-1110	Cash	$5,000.00	
	3-1000	Paid-in Capital		$5,000.00
12/31/Year 1	#2 - Bob buys a truck.			
	1-2100	Truck - Original Cost	$15,000.00	
	2-2100	Note Payable - Truck Loan		$15,000.00
12/31/Year 1	#3 - Bob goes shopping.			
	1-1800	Inventory	$3,000.00	
	1-1110	Cash		$3,000.00
12/31/Year 1	#4 - Bob sells a hosebib.			
	4-1000	Sales		$150.00
	1-1110	Cash	$150.00	
	5-1000	Materials	$95.00	
	1-1800	Inventory		$95.00
		Grand Total:	$23,245.00	$23,245.00

EAGLE PLUMBING COMPANY
GENERAL LEDGER
DETAIL TRIAL BALANCE

12/31/YEAR 1

Date Memo	Debit	Credit	Net Activity	Ending Balance
1-1110 Cash		Beginning Balance:	$0.00	
12/31/Year 1 #1 - Bob takes money from	$5,000.00			$5,000.00
12/31/Year 1 #3 - Bob goes shopping.		$3,000.00		$2,000.00
12/31/Year 1 #4 - Bob sells a hosebib.	$150.00			$2,150.00
Total:	$5,150.00	$3,000.00	$2,150.00	$2,150.00
1-1800 Inventory		Beginning Balance:	$0.00	
12/31/Year 1 #3 - Bob goes shopping.	$3,000.00			$3,000.00
12/31/Year 1 #4 - Bob sells a hosebib.		$95.00		$2,905.00
Total:	$3,000.00	$95.00	$2,905.00	$2,905.00
1-2100 Truck - Original Cost		Beginning Balance:	$0.00	
12/31/Year 1 #2 - Bob buys a truck.	$15,000.00			$15,000.00
Total:	$15,000.00	$0.00	$15,000.00	$15,000.00
2-2100 Note Payable - Truck Loan		Beginning Balance:	$0.00	
12/31/Year 1 #2 - Bob buys a truck.		$15,000.00		$15,000.00 cr
Total:	$0.00	$15,000.00	$15,000.00 cr	$15,000.00 cr
3-1000 Paid-in Capital		Beginning Balance:	$0.00	
12/31/Year 1 #1 - Bob takes money from		$5,000.00		$5,000.00 cr
Total:	$0.00	$5,000.00	$5,000.00 cr	$5,000.00 cr
4-1000 Sales		Beginning Balance:	$0.00	
12/31/Year 1 #4 - Bob sells a hosebib.		$150.00		$150.00 cr
Total:	$0.00	$150.00	$150.00 cr	$150.00 cr
5-1000 Materials		Beginning Balance:	$0.00	
12/31/Year 1 #4 - Bob sells a hosebib.	$95.00			$95.00
Total:	$95.00	$0.00	$95.00	$95.00

Grand Total: $23,245.00 $23,245.00

Transaction #5

BOB SELLS A WATER HEATER, INCLUDING INSTALLATION.

 Let's work out another Sales transaction on the Balance Sheet and Income Statement. Just as he is wrapping up with Fred, the phone rings. A real customer this time! Mrs. Lawson is a sweet old lady. She saw Bob's truck buzzing past her house and decided she would call. Her old water heater had started to leak and she figured it might need to be replaced. Gosh, it had to be at least 15 years old. She moved into this home that many years ago, and she had never had any work done on the water heater.

Bob rushes to Mrs. Lawson's House and tries to dazzle her with his expertise and devotion to customer service. In fact Bob chatters on and on about his skills and licenses and his promises to be there in a flash should anything ever go wrong. Mrs. Lawson is smiling and nodding. Bob thinks she is agreeing to everything he is recommending. Really, she is very hard of hearing. He offers to install an new water heater. Bob paid $160 for the water heater when he stocked his truck. As he did before, he makes up a selling price.

Now, just to make it easy on us, let's say Bob accurately calculates the cost of his wages including all benefits to be $45 per hour. He predicts, based on past experience that it will take him a total of 3 hours to replace the heater, including all travel time and clean up. He pays himself a total of $135 for his work as a technician. Bob also needs to get a $15 permit for the job.

Aiming high Bob pulls a selling price of $450 — he remembers Turkey Drain Cleaning would charge $475 for the same heater — and scribbles it on an invoice. Mrs. Lawson nods and smiles and writes a check for $450. Although she couldn't understand much of what he was saying, she knows he brought a water heater with him. If she writes a check he can get to work…and then she won't have to pretend to listen to him anymore! Let's record this transaction on the Income Statement and Balance Sheet. We know this...

Labor cost is: 3 hours @ $45.00 per hour = $135.00

Material Cost is: $160.00

Permit Fee is: $15.00

Total cost is $310 and. . . Bob charges $450.00 for the job.

Income Statement…after both transactions. Compare to Income Statement on page 40. Note the changes.

EAGLE PLUMBING COMPANY
INCOME STATEMENT
AFTER BOTH SALES TRANSACTIONS

12/31/YEAR 1

Income		
Sales	$600.00	
Total Income		$600.00
Direct Costs		
Materials	$255.00	
Billable Labor	$135.00	
Permits	$15.00	
Total Direct Costs		$405.00
Gross Profit		$195.00
Net Profit/(Loss)		$195.00

EAGLE PLUMBING COMPANY
BALANCE SHEET

DECEMBER YEAR 1

Assets			
Current Assets			
Cash	$2,450.00		
Inventory	$2,745.00		
Total Current Assets		$5,195.00	
Vehicles			
Truck - Original Cost	$15,000.00		
Total Vehicles		$15,000.00	
Total Assets			$20,195.00
Liabilities			
Long Term Liabilities			
Note Payable - Truck Loan	$15,000.00		
Total Long Term Liabilities		$15,000.00	
Total Liabilities			$15,000.00
Equity			
Paid-in Capital		$5,000.00	
Current Year Earnings		$195.00	
Total Equity			$5,195.00
Total Liability & Equity			$20,195.00

Accounts

Cash	
$5000 (#1)	$3000 (#3)
$150 (#4)	$135 (#5)
$450 (#5)	$15 (#5)
Bal: $2450	

Loan	
	$15000 (#2)

Truck	
$15000 (#2)	

Paid In Capital	
	$5000 (#1)

Inventory	
$3000 (#3)	$95 (#4)
	$160 (#5)
Bal: $2745	

Sales	
	$150 (#4)
	$450 (#5)
	Bal: $600

Note: We could have listed material, labor and permit costs under separate accounts. I lumped them together as Direct Costs to keep it simple.

Direct Costs	
$95 (#4)	
$160 (#5)	
$135 (#5)	
$15 (#5)	
Bal: $405	

EAGLE PLUMBING COMPANY

JOURNAL

12/31/YEAR 1

Date	Account #	Account Name	Debit	Credit
12/31/Year 1	#1 - Bob takes money from under his mattress.			
	1-1110	Cash	$5,000.00	
	3-1000	Paid-in Capital		$5,000.00
12/31/Year 1	#2 - Bob buys a truck.			
	1-2100	Truck - Original Cost	$15,000.00	
	2-2100	Note Payable - Truck Loan		$15,000.00
12/31/Year 1	#3 - Bob goes shopping.			
	1-1800	Inventory	$3,000.00	
	1-1110	Cash		$3,000.00
12/31/Year 1	#4 - Bob sells a hosebib.			
	4-1000	Sales		$150.00
	1-1110	Cash	$150.00	
	5-1000	Materials	$95.00	
	1-1800	Inventory		$95.00
12/31/Year 1	#5 - Bob sells a water heater, including installation.			
	5-1000	Materials	$160.00	
	1-1800	Inventory		$160.00
	5-2000	Billable Labor	$135.00	
	1-1110	Cash		$135.00
	4-1000	Sales		$450.00
	1-1110	Cash	$450.00	
	5-3000	Permits	$15.00	
	1-1110	Cash		$15.00
		Grand Total:	$24,005.00	$24,005.00

EAGLE PLUMBING COMPANY
GENERAL LEDGER
DETAIL TRIAL BALANCE

12/31/YEAR 1

Date	Memo	Debit	Credit	Net Activity	Ending Balance
1-1110 Cash			Beginning Balance:	$0.00	
12/31/Year 1 #1 - Bob takes money from		$5,000.00			$5,000.00
12/31/Year 1 #3 - Bob goes shopping.			$3,000.00		$2,000.00
12/31/Year 1 #4 - Bob sells a hosebib.		$150.00			$2,150.00
12/31/Year 1 #5 - Bob sells a water heater.			$135.00		$2,015.00
12/31/Year 1 #5 - Bob sells a water heater.		$450.00			$2,465.00
12/31/Year 1 #5 - Bob sells a water heater.			$15.00		$2,450.00
	Total:	$5,600.00	$3,150.00	$2,450.00	$2,450.00
1-1800 Inventory			Beginning Balance:	$0.00	
12/31/Year 1 #3 - Bob goes shopping.		$3,000.00			$3,000.00
12/31/Year 1 #4 - Bob sells a hosebib.			$95.00		$2,905.00
12/31/Year 1 #5 - Bob sells a water heater			$160.00		$2,745.00
	Total:	$3,000.00	$255.00	$2,745.00	$2,745.00
1-2100 Truck - Original Cost			Beginning Balance:	$0.00	
12/31/Year 1 #2 - Bob buys a truck.		$15,000.00			$15,000.00
	Total:	$15,000.00	$0.00	$15,000.00	$15,000.00
2-2100 Note Payable - Truck Loan			Beginning Balance:	$0.00	
12/31/Year 1 #2 - Bob buys a truck.			$15,000.00		$15,000.00 cr
	Total:	$0.00	$15,000.00	$15,000.00 cr	$15,000.00 cr
3-1000 Paid-in Capital			Beginning Balance:	$0.00	
12/31/Year 1 #1 - Bob takes money from			$5,000.00		$5,000.00 cr
	Total:	$0.00	$5,000.00	$5,000.00 cr	$5,000.00 cr
4-1000 Sales			Beginning Balance:	$0.00	
12/31/Year 1 #4 - Bob sells a hosebib.			$150.00		$150.00 cr
12/31/Year 1 #5 - Bob sells a water heater.			$450.00		$600.00 cr
	Total:	$0.00	$600.00	$600.00 cr	$600.00 cr
5-1000 Materials			Beginning Balance:	$0.00	
12/31/Year 1 #4 - Bob sells a hosebib.		$95.00			$95.00
12/31/Year 1 #5 - Bob sells a water heater.		$160.00			$255.00
	Total:	$255.00	$0.00	$255.00	$255.00
5-2000 Billable Labor			Beginning Balance:	$0.00	
12/31/Year 1 #5 - Bob sells a water heater.		$135.00			$135.00
	Total:	$135.00	$0.00	$135.00	$135.00
5-3000 Permits			Beginning Balance:	$0.00	
12/31/Year 1 #5 - Bob sells a water heater.		$15.00			$15.00
	Total:	$15.00	$0.00	$15.00	$15.00
	Grand Total:	$24,005.00	$24,005.00		

WOW! EAGLE PLUMBING IS KICKING BUTT!
THIS BUSINESS *BUSINESS* IS EASY!

However....If this was all there was to it, then the world would be full of prosperous businesses. How could you lose??

In reality most business fail...breaking their owners in the process. What happens???

Most business owners don't understand and account for the **Indirect Costs** of doing business when they set selling prices!!

There are **Direct Costs** (Job Site Expenses, Cost of Goods Sold) and **Indirect Costs** (Overhead)

While Bob is out selling and plumbing, bills are being delivered to his home office...telephone, printing, yellow page ads, insurance. Bob's Income Statement needs to be expanded to include ALL the Expenses associated with doing business. In reality, there are a lot of expenses involved in running Eagle Plumbing. Bob is aware of the Materials, Labor and Permit. These expenses are *directly* related to a specific job. They are Job Site Expenses, Cost of Goods Sold or Direct Costs.

The other expenses involved in operating the company are Overhead, or Indirect Costs. These expenses are *indirectly* related to jobs. Indirect Costs include advertising, insurance, office expenses, donations, truck repairs...the list goes on. These costs are often overlooked or discounted by folks who don't look at their Financials.

In fact, it is likely that Eagle Plumbing's Indirect Costs exceed the Direct Costs. Unless Bob takes a look at his *total* costs of doing business, his out-of-the-blue selling prices will sink his company. After a few months of operating, the indirect costs will take all of Bob's cash...and take him farther in debt. Bob will shake his head and wonder...

"Where did the money go?"

If you are a banker or an accountant, I might ruffle your feathers here ...brace yourself!

Bob priced the hosebib $55 over his direct cost of the item. Was this a good move? Did he make any money? Bob just pulled that selling price out of thin air.

When business owners make up selling prices, they trot out this silly phrase as their reasoning: *I charge what the market will bear.* Sadly, virtually all business literature, and most accountants and bankers, will back up the going rate theory. You will be instructed to establish a selling price that is within a percentage point or two of what everyone else in the market is charging.

May I suggest that if most businesses fail — about 80% in the first three years — it is foolish to base your financial well being on what others are charging. What makes you think the fellow down the road has any idea what he is doing? Sure he is busy…busy isn't so hard. Creating and sustaining profits and developing careers for you and your staff…ah, there's the rub.

THIS IS WHY I WROTE THIS BOOK!

When creating selling prices, base them on your real costs of doing business, including fair compensation for you and your hardworking employees…NOT ON WHAT THE MARKET WILL BEAR.

Consider what the market will bear… $20,000 for a Rolex watch, $125 for a cigarette lighter, $4 for a six pack of soda. The market is not strictly price driven…or even primarily price driven.

This is what it takes to make money in your business:
- ▲ Develop a fair price based on your costs.
- ▲ Present your products in such a way that *value* outweighs price.

Why is this *what the market will bear* nonsense so ingrained? Ignorant men will defer to the opinion of experts. **Some experts in accounting will tell you silly rules like**:
- ▲ Take your cost of product and double it to create a selling price.
- ▲ Find out what others in your industry are charging, and then charge less.
- ▲ If you are not making any money, cut down on your expenses.

These suggestions are not based on facts. You need to know what your *costs* are, then create a selling price that will cover all costs plus profit.

THE DIFFERENCE BETWEEN MANAGERIAL ACCOUNTING AND "UNCLE SAM" ACCOUNTING

My savvy friend Manola Robison has a nice way to help you understand the difference between the kind of accounting that the government needs to see on your tax returns and the kind of accounting that will give you the information you need to run your business.

Manola says, "Your accountant wants to make sure you comply with IRS regulations. There are rules you must follow with "Uncle Sam" Accounting. By the time your accountant has ensured that your Financials are ready for "Uncle Sam" they are old news. "Uncle Sam" accounting has an 'outside' orientation, meaning that the Financials are generated for the government and bankers. Managerial Accounting has an 'inside' orientation. This financial information is generated to help you manage your company. You want news hot off the press so you can make informed decisions as quickly as possible."

I'm not suggesting the ol' 'two sets of books' here!! Your Managerial information is not at odds with the "Uncle Sam" information. Rather, it is quickly gathered and analyzed for in-house management. The "Uncle Sam" version waits for the dust to settle from the previous month, and focuses on tax law compliance.

Here's a nice illustration of the difference between Managerial information and "Uncle Sam" accounting... Your accountant will structure your Income Statement to determine profits before taxes. Why? Because that is the information he uses to determine what your tax liability is! You, however, also need to look at post tax profit. Is it enough? How much do you need to charge to make it all work? What changes can you make today? Make sure your 'inside' accounting gives you the information you need.

Taxes are a cost of doing business and need to be figured into the selling price of your services. If I had a dollar for every time I've heard a contractor say, "I was doing really well this year, but, then the IRS took it all!" You can only guess at many costs when you look into the future. But TAXES? Count on them, for crying out loud. And price accordingly.

SEPARATING INDIRECT COSTS FROM DIRECT COSTS IS A MANAGERIAL ACCOUNTING DECISION.

Left to his own devices, your accountant will probably list all the expenses of the company in one section below Sales in the Income Statement. Maybe he separates the Material and calls it Cost of Good Sold. But this information is too vague and general to use for decision making in your company. Let's add more accounts to the Income Statement to gather more information.

Income Statement	
Sales	$600
Direct Costs	
Materials	255
Labor including all benefits	135
Permits	15
Gross Margin	195
Indirect Costs	
Owner's Salary including all benefits	
Non–billable Labor including all benefits	
Advertising	
Depreciation	
Truck Maintenance & Repair	
Tools	
Education	
Professional Services	
Insurance	
Uniforms	
Office Supplies	
Taxes	
Profit	$195

"What about these costs?" No activity yet, be patient.

There could be many more categories for expenses. We'll keep it simple in this illustration to make the concepts easy to understand.

49

Notice that the Expenses have been divided into two categories...Direct Costs and Indirect Costs. Let's define the terms:

Direct Costs (a.k.a. Cost of Goods Sold, Cost of Sales or Job Site Expenses): These expenses are *directly* related to a sale. If the sale didn't happen, the expense would not be incurred. Direct Costs refers to material, labor costs and permits used at a specific jobsite. Or, the cost of the item you purchased intending to resell it.

If a tool was purchased to be used on a specific job and it was used to the point of complete depreciation on that job, then you would include that tool as a Direct Cost. If you bought a tool to be used on lots of different jobs it would not be a Direct Cost. It would be an *Indirect Cost*.

Most business owners understand Direct Costs and charge their customers enough to cover these costs. It's the Indirect Costs that get overlooked.

Indirect Costs (a.k.a. Operating Expenses or Overhead): Every expense *other* than the Direct Costs. These are the costs you need to operate the business every day, to keep a roof *overhead*. They are *indirectly* related to sales. These costs remain fairly constant whether you have lots of sales, or sales are down.

An example of an Indirect Cost is the telephone bill. If Bob Bird had no sales this day, well, the telephone expense would still be incurred. Indirect Costs can't be assigned to a specific job. To what job do you assign the copy machine repairs? Get the idea?

Each selling price should be calculated to include a *portion* of your entire Indirect Costs burden. It would not make sense to hit up Mr. Jones for your entire rent payment.

Why is it helpful to separate the Indirect Costs from the Direct Costs? As a manager, you need to know how much money it takes to cover Indirect Costs every month. Busy or slow, Indirect Costs are racking up, hour by hour. How much does it take to 'crack the nut' each month? Without sales, Direct Costs go away — no problem. Ah, but not so with the Indirect Costs...you better know how much you need to run your company.

Indirect Costs include owner's salary. Why? Well, the owner is entitled to compensation for the administrative functions he performs in the company. Bob can put on his technician uniform and earn wages in the field. Those wages are Direct Costs. As the owner-manager Bob needs a salary that compensates his work as a manager. His owner's salary is an Indirect Cost.

Look again at the Income Statement. Notice that after you subtract Direct Costs from Sales you arrive at *Gross Margin*.

Gross Margin (a.k.a. Gross Profit): Now, I don't like the term Gross Profit. It leads folks to think they may have some real profits at this point and that may not be the case. So, I prefer Gross Margin.

At the Gross Margin point, you subtract the Indirect Costs to find Net Profit. If your Gross Margin is really solid, you may have enough to cover all Indirect Costs and generate respectable profit. How much Gross Margin is enough? As you become proactive with your company's Financials, you will understand what you need to achieve your goals.

Net Profit (a.k.a. Net Earnings or Net Income): This is the 'bottom line.' This is the real profit figure after ALL expenses have been deducted. This is my favorite statistic.

You'll remember that this figure connects the Income Statement to the Balance Sheet. The Net Profit dollar amount is the Current Earnings dollar amount. As the Income Statement is really a look at the change that takes place in the Equity section of the Balance Sheet, the Net Profit is the 'net change' in Equity.

"But wait a minute. I am not a plumber! I sell T-shirts!"

As an example company, I created Eagle Plumbing. Eagle Plumbing is a typical service company. This company is much like any business that 'sells' their expertise, or *time*. Doctors, consultants, lawyers, tradespeople, and contractors to name a few.

But what if you sell strictly products...like T-shirts? I suggest this model will still work for you. The reality is your shop has only so much time every day to make sales.

• •

A BRIEF LECTURE ON WHY YOU NEED PROFIT *AND* OWNER'S SALARY

Most business owners mistakenly believe that they will gather up all the profit left over at the end of the year, stuff it in their pockets and consider themselves compensated. Wrong!

The company is a separate, living, growing entity. Profit fuels your company's growth. If you choose to buy a new building, or buy a company to do Air Conditioning work, you finance the company's growth with profit. You can share profit with your employees via a profit-sharing plan. As the owner, Bob is entitled to a return on investment for his risk and exposure as an investor. Cool, huh?

Your salary compensates you for the headache, heartache, time, risk and energy you put into the company. Your salary provides for you and your family. You need BOTH profit and salary. Enough said.

• •

Back to the Income Statement…

Let's take a look at the duties that Bob Bird performs at Eagle Plumbing. Sometimes he is doing service work, other times he is performing administrative tasks. His time should be split up into Direct and Indirect Costs.

What your accountant won't tell you. Determining the Billable Hour.

Unless you purposefully train your accountant to do otherwise, he will lump all Payroll expenses together. But, sometimes you are 'turning wrenches' or selling. Sometimes you are running for parts, cleaning up, training or standing by. You're limited to what you can sell based on the number of labor hours you have. To understand what's happening in your business, you need to know how much time you are generating sales compared to all your other duties.

You need to track your employees' time as well. Using our service company example, suppose the service technicians are *available* for calls 8 hours a day, 5 days a week, a total of 40 hours each. Of those 40 hours, each tech will generate some time for which you are able to bill the customer via an invoice. The hours that are billable to the customer are called **Billable Hours.**

"Hey…I pay strictly on commission. Why do I need to worry about Billable Hours? I don't pay the techs if they don't sell."

Whether your pay structure is commission based or hourly, you still need to know the number of hours Billable, and compare to the hours not Billable. There are only 24 hours in a day. Of those, your service providers are only available for a fixed number of hours. That's all the time you have to recover all the Indirect (Overhead) costs that your company generates every day.

If you pay on a commission basis, you don't pay the service providers for non-Billable hours. That's fine. BUT, you're not home free. Your rent, advertising, administrative costs, etc., are still racking up. Your company's survival depends on a minimum number of Billable hours.

Most state labor laws will still require you to keep track of the total hours put in by your people. Also, you can't help them get better and more efficient if you don't measure their performance!

If you sell services by the hour…**The number of Billable Hours at your company is the variable with the biggest impact on your Financial Statements.**

Let's use Bob Bird and Eagle Plumbing Co. to help us understand the impact of Billable hours:

Transaction #6

BOB FILLS OUT HIS TIMESHEET.

At Eagle Plumbing, the only employee is Bob. He wears a lot of hats…customer service representative, dispatcher, bookkeeper, technician, warehouse manager. Although Bob HATES paperwork, he has filled in his time card. I'm so glad because this data is so critical. Take a look at his time card.

Timesheet for Eagle Plumbing		
Name: Bob Bird	Date: 12/31/Year 1	
Hours	**Activity**	**Billable?**
2	hosebib	no
3	water heater	yes
1	sweep shop, wash truck	no
2	phone, bids	no

Assume Bob will only work at Eagle 8 hours a day (Ha!). He has calculated his hourly cost including benefits to be $45 per hour for any task he is performing for the company. Of 8 available hours, Bob had 3 Billable hours — the water heater installation.

Bonus Question: Should the 2 hours that Bob spent with Fred and the hosebib be considered Billable hours? Is travel time Billable time? An argument could be made for calling these hours Billable…that's fine. The key is being *consistent* with your data.

So, for this example let's agree that the other 5 hours are not Billable. However, the customer pays for this time as well. How? Hang on…we're getting there.

Let's record Bob's pay on the Income Statement and Balance Sheet using the timesheet information. We had already paid Bob for his Direct Labor Cost. We just need to account for the Indirect Cost of his Owner's Salary. This is what the Financials look like now….to keep it simple, we are including all taxes in the $45 per hour figure.

Let's consider the five hours that Bob spent doing other tasks at Eagle Plumbing. For simplicity we'll put all five hours in Indirect Cost- owner's salary. Bob decides to compensate himself as the owner for those five hours. (5 X $45 = $225)

Income Statement

Sales	$600
Direct Costs	
Materials	255
Labor including all benefits	135
Permits	15
Gross Margin	195
Indirect Costs	
Owner's Salary including all benefits	225
Non–billable Labor	
Advertising	
Depreciation	
Truck Maintenance & Repair	
Tools	
Education	
Professional Services	
Insurance	
Uniforms	
Office Supplies	
Taxes	
Profit	($30)

"We still haven't accounted for these expenses. Don't worry, we will!

EAGLE PLUMBING COMPANY
PROFIT & LOSS STATEMENT

DECEMBER 31, YEAR 1

Income		
Sales	$600.00	
Total Income		$600.00
Direct Costs		
Materials	$255.00	
Billable Labor	$135.00	
Permits	$15.00	
Total Direct Costs		$405.00
Gross Profit		$195.00
Indirect Costs		
Owner's Salary	$225.00	
Total Indirect Costs		$225.00
Net Profit		($30.00)

EAGLE PLUMBING COMPANY
BALANCE SHEET
DECEMBER 31, YEAR 1

Assets
  Current Assets
    Cash $2,225.00
    Inventory $2,745.00
  Total Current Assets $4,970.00
  Vehicles
    Truck - Original Cost $15,000.00
  Total Vehicles $15,000.00
Total Assets $19,970.00

Liabilities
  Long Term Liabilities
    Note Payable - Truck Loan $15,000.00
  Total Long Term Liabilities $15,000.00
Total Liabilities $15,000.00

Equity
  Paid-in Capital $5,000.00
  Current Year Earnings   ($30.00)
  Total Equity $4,970.00

Total Liability & Equity $19,970.00

Accounts after Transaction #6.

Cash

$5000 (#1)	$3000 (#3)
$150 (#4)	$135 (#5)
$450 (#5)	$15 (#5)
	$225 (#6)

Bal: $2225

Truck

$15000 (#2)	

Inventory

$3000 (#3)	$95 (#4)
	$160 (#5)
Bal: $2745	

Loan

	$15000 (#2)

Sales

	$150 (#4)
	$450 (#5)
	Bal: $600

Paid In Capital

	$5000 (#1)

Direct Costs

$95 (#4)	
$160 (#5)	
$135 (#5)	
$15 (#5)	
Bal: $405	

Owner's Salary

$225 (#6)	

EAGLE PLUMBING COMPANY

JOURNAL

12/31/YEAR 1

Date	Account #	Account Name	Debit	Credit
12/31/Year 1	#1 - Bob takes money from under his mattress.			
	1-1110	Cash	$5,000.00	
	3-1000	Paid-in Capital		$5,000.00
12/31/Year 1	#2 - Bob buys a truck.			
	1-2100	Truck - Original Cost	$15,000.00	
	2-2100	Note Payable - Truck Loan		$15,000.00
12/31/Year 1	#3 - Bob goes shopping.			
	1-1800	Inventory	$3,000.00	
	1-1110	Cash		$3,000.00
12/31/Year 1	#4 - Bob sells a hosebib.			
	4-1000	Sales		$150.00
	1-1110	Cash	$150.00	
	5-1000	Materials	$95.00	
	1-1800	Inventory		$95.00
12/31/Year 1	#5 - Bob sells a water heater, including installation.			
	5-1000	Materials	$160.00	
	1-1800	Inventory		$160.00
	5-2000	Billable Labor	$135.00	
	1-1110	Cash		$135.00
	4-1000	Sales		$450.00
	1-1110	Cash	$450.00	
	5-3000	Permits	$15.00	
	1-1110	Cash		$15.00
12/31/Year 1	#6 - Bob fills out his time sheet.			
	6-1000	Owner's Salary	$225.00	
	1-1110	Cash		$225.00
		Grand Total:	$24,230.00	$24,230.00

57

EAGLE PLUMBING COMPANY
GENERAL LEDGER
DETAIL TRIAL BALANCE

12/31/YEAR 1

Date	Memo	Debit	Credit	Net Activity	Ending Balance
1-1110 Cash			Beginning Balance:	$0.00	
12/31/Year 1 #1 - Bob takes money from		$5,000.00			$5,000.00
12/31/Year 1 #3 - Bob goes shopping.			$3,000.00		$2,000.00
12/31/Year 1 #4 - Bob sells a hosebib.		$150.00			$2,150.00
12/31/Year 1 #5 - Bob sells a water heater.			$135.00		$2,015.00
12/31/Year 1 #5 - Bob sells a water heater.		$450.00			$2,465.00
12/31/Year 1 #5 - Bob sells a water heater.			$15.00		$2,450.00
12/31/Year 1 #6 - Bob fills out his time sheet.			$225.00		$2,225.00
	Total:	$5,600.00	$3,375.00	$2,225.00	$2,225.00
1-1800 Inventory			Beginning Balance:	$0.00	
12/31/Year 1 #3 - Bob goes shopping.		$3,000.00			$3,000.00
12/31/Year 1 #4 - Bob sells a hosebib.			$95.00		$2,905.00
12/31/Year 1 #5 - Bob sells a water heater			$160.00		$2,745.00
	Total:	$3,000.00	$255.00	$2,745.00	$2,745.00
1-2100 Truck - Original Cost			Beginning Balance:	$0.00	
12/31/Year 1 #2 - Bob buys a truck.		$15,000.00			$15,000.00
	Total:	$15,000.00	$0.00	$15,000.00	$15,000.00
2-2100 Note Payable - Truck Loan			Beginning Balance:	$0.00	
12/31/Year 1 #2 - Bob buys a truck.			$15,000.00		$15,000.00 cr
	Total:	$0.00	$15,000.00	$15,000.00 cr	$15,000.00 cr
3-1000 Paid-in Capital			Beginning Balance:	$0.00	
12/31/Year 1 #1 - Bob takes money from			$5,000.00		$5,000.00 cr
	Total:	$0.00	$5,000.00	$5,000.00 cr	$5,000.00 cr
4-1000 Sales			Beginning Balance:	$0.00	
12/31/Year 1 #4 - Bob sells a hosebib.			$150.00		$150.00 cr
12/31/Year 1 #5 - Bob sells a water heater.			$450.00		$600.00 cr
	Total:	$0.00	$600.00	$600.00 cr	$600.00 cr
5-1000 Materials			Beginning Balance:	$0.00	
12/31/Year 1 #4 - Bob sells a hosebib.		$95.00			$95.00
12/31/Year 1 #5 - Bob sells a water heater.		$160.00			$255.00
	Total:	$255.00	$0.00	$255.00	$255.00
5-2000 Billable Labor			Beginning Balance:	$0.00	
12/31/Year 1 #5 - Bob sells a water heater.		$135.00			$135.00
	Total:	$135.00	$0.00	$135.00	$135.00
5-3000 Permits			Beginning Balance:	$0.00	
12/31/Year 1 #5 - Bob sells a water heater.		$15.00			$15.00
	Total:	$15.00	$0.00	$15.00	$15.00
6-1000 Owner's Salary			Beginning Balance:	$0.00	
12/31/Year 1 #6 - Bob fills out timesheet.		$225.00			$225.00
	Total:	$225.00	$0.00	$225.00	$225.00
	Grand Total:	$24,230.00	$24,230.00		

MORE ON THE TIMESHEET

Question for Discussion: How do you determine your Billable Hours? Take a minute to think about how you can apply this concept to your business.

_____

_____

_____

_____

If you are a service company, you need to look at the daily timesheets and the number of hours billed via the invoice. Remember to compare the number of hours spent on a job to the number of hours _billed_ on that job. (If you have a computer system that can help with this task, fine. If not, use a columnar pad or a simple spreadsheet program.)

"I CAN NAME THAT TUNE IN THREE NOTES!"

Remember that TV game show? The contestants, full of competitive enthusiasm, would try to identify a song in the fewest possible notes. Of course you want to perform any task that you do in the minimum amount of time. But beware of creating selling prices that are based on the 'ideal scene. ' It is realistic to have some inefficiencies in the service business.

Suppose that when Bob Bird went to Mrs. Lawson's house he accidentally let her pet daschund out of the backyard. It could have taken an hour to round the dog up. While I don't suggest you assume that all heck will break loose on every job, you do want to include some extra minutes in your calculations.

If you sell only products, keep track of the number of hours that your salespeople are actively selling. As you track all your costs of doing business, direct and indirect, you will be able to determine the amount of sales per hour you will need to break even — and make a profit.

"I CAN MAKE IT UP IN MATERIALS.!"

Can you charge $50 per Billable Labor Hour and make up the difference in Material?? Assuming you are a service provider, if your customers were looking for material only, would they call you? Can you compete with a warehouse supplier or home center on a straight material sale?

In the previous example Bob sold a hosebib, parts only. However, isn't it more realistic that Bob would be asked to install the hosebib...even if the homeowner got the part from someone else? His value in the marketplace is his ability to INSTALL, not supply, the material.

You can generate profits from material sales. But, I recommend that service providers price to *cover your Overhead* via the Billable Labor Hour. Cover your assets. That way, if you don't get the material sale, you still win.

Are you willing to lose money on every low material job? If not, price your Billable Hour to cover all costs and generate profit. Then all material sales are gravy.

Your customers value your ability to put the "derned thing in" or figure out the problem! The primary "widget" in the service industry is the Billable Hour.

After all, Bob can't sell and install 15 water heaters in a single day. He only has 24 hours! If you could sell unlimited materials, this would be a different discussion. But installed materials impose labor hours…and you only have so many labor hours per tech, per day.

If you run a retail outlet, your material sales could generate enough money to cover all expenses, including salaries and compensation and a nice profit. BUT, you are still limited by TIME…**how many hours a day is the store open to sell**? Perhaps could break even by selling 5,000 T-shirts. *But could you sell that many? Could you have that many on hand?* Could that many people want them? How much TIME would it take to generate sales of 5,000 shirts? Your selling price must always take the TIME factor into account. This book is written specifically for folks who sell services by the hour BUT the concepts can be expanded to any business.

Transaction #7

BOB ACCOUNTS FOR HIS OVERHEAD EXPENSES.

Good ol' Bob has seen the light. He knows that there is more to running the business than he first imagined. The first thing he must do is get realistic about how much his company is costing to run each day. Bob realizes that he is incurring all kinds of expenses other than the Direct Costs of Labor and Materials. (Atta boy, Bob!) So he makes a list of all the bills he pays over the course of the year. The Chart of Accounts can be a handy tool for this. Let's assume for the sake of our educational experience today that Bob accurately accounts for one day's worth of Overhead expenses. What does this do to the Financials?

EAGLE PLUMBING COMPANY
PROFIT & LOSS STATEMENT

DECEMBER 31, YEAR 1

Income			
Sales	$600.00		100.0%
Total Income		$600.00	100.0%
Direct Costs			
Materials	$255.00		42.5%
Billable Labor	$135.00		22.5%
Permits	$15.00		2.5%
Total Direct Costs		$405.00	67.5%
Gross Profit		$195.00	32.5%
Indirect Costs			
Owner's Salary	$225.00		37.5%
Advertising	$35.00		5.8%
Education	$5.00		.8%
Insurance	$10.00		1.7%
Office Supplies	$10.00		1.7%
Professional Services	$25.00		4.2%
Tools	$15.00		2.5%
Truck Maintenance & Repair	$30.00		5.0%
Uniforms	$20.00		3.3%
Total Indirect Costs		$375.00	62.5%
Net Profit / (Loss)		($180.00)	(30.0%)

EAGLE PLUMBING COMPANY
BALANCE SHEET
DECEMBER 31, YEAR 1

Assets
  Current Assets
    Cash $2,075.00
    Inventory $2,745.00
  Total Current Assets $4,820.00
  Vehicles
    Truck - Original Cost $15,000.00
  Total Vehicles $15,000.00
Total Assets $19,820.00

Liabilities
  Long Term Liabilities
    Note Payable - Truck Loan $15,000.00
  Total Long Term Liabilities $15,000.00
Total Liabilities $15,000.00

Equity
  Paid-in Capital $5,000.00
  Current Year Earnings   ($180.00)
  Total Equity $4,820.00

Total Liability & Equity $19,820.00

Accounts after transaction #7.

Cash

$5000 (#1)	$3000 (#3)
$150 (#4)	$135 (#5)
$450 (#5)	$15 (#5)
	$225 (#6)
	$35 (#7)
	$5 (#7)
	$10 (#7)
	$10 (#7)
	$25 (#7)
	$15 (#7)
	$30 (#7)
	$20 (#7)
Bal: $2075	

Loan

	$15000 (#2)

Sales

	$150 (#4)
	$450 (#5)
	Bal: $600

Truck	
$15000 (#2)	

Paid In Capital	
	$5000 (#1)

Inventory	
$3000 (#3)	$95 (#4)
	$160 (#5)
Bal: $2745	

Direct Costs	
$95 (#4)	
$160 (#5)	
$135 (#5)	
$15 (#5)	

Tools	
$15 (#7)	

Owner's Salary	
$225 (#6)	

Office Supplies	
$10 (#7)	

Uniforms	
$20 (#7)	

Education	
$5 (#7)	

Advertising	
$35 (#7)	

Insurance	
$10 (#7)	

Professional Services	
$25 (#7)	

Truck Maintenance	
$30 (#7)	

EAGLE PLUMBING COMPANY
JOURNAL
12/31/YEAR 1

Date	Account #	Account Name	Debit	Credit
12/31/Year 1	#1 - Bob takes money from under his mattress.			
	1-1110	Cash	$5,000.00	
	3-1000	Paid-in Capital		$5,000.00
12/31/Year 1	#2 - Bob buys a truck.			
	1-2100	Truck - Original Cost	$15,000.00	
	2-2100	Note Payable - Truck Loan		$15,000.00
12/31/Year 1	#3 - Bob goes shopping.			
	1-1800	Inventory	$3,000.00	
	1-1110	Cash		$3,000.00
12/31/Year 1	#4 - Bob sells a hosebib.			
	4-1000	Sales		$150.00
	1-1110	Cash	$150.00	
	5-1000	Materials	$95.00	
	1-1800	Inventory		$95.00
12/31/Year 1	#5 - Bob sells a water heater, including installation.			
	5-1000	Materials	$160.00	
	1-1800	Inventory		$160.00
	5-2000	Billable Labor	$135.00	
	1-1110	Cash		$135.00
	4-1000	Sales		$450.00
	1-1110	Cash	$450.00	
	5-3000	Permits	$15.00	
	1-1110	Cash		$15.00
12/31/Year 1	#6 - Bob fills out his time sheet.			
	6-1000	Owner's Salary	$225.00	
	1-1110	Cash		$225.00
12/31/Year 1	#5 - Bob accounts for his overhead expenses.			
	6-2000	Advertising	$35.00	
	6-3000	Education	$5.00	
	6-3050	Insurance	$10.00	
	6-4000	Office Supplies	$10.00	
	6-4050	Professional Services	$25.00	
	6-5000	Tools	$15.00	
	6-5050	Truck Maintenance & Repair	$30.00	
	6-6000	Uniforms	$20.00	
	1-1110	Cash		$150.00
		Grand Total:	$24,380.00	$24,380.00

EAGLE PLUMBING COMPANY
GENERAL LEDGER
DETAIL TRIAL BALANCE

12/31/YEAR 1

Date	Memo	Debit	Credit	Net Activity	Ending Balance
1-1110 Cash			Beginning Balance:	$0.00	
12/31/Year 1 #1 - Bob takes money from		$5,000.00			$5,000.00
12/31/Year 1 #3 - Bob goes shopping.			$3,000.00		$2,000.00
12/31/Year 1 #4 - Bob sells a hosebib.		$150.00			$2,150.00
12/31/Year 1 #5 - Bob sells a water heater.			$135.00		$2,015.00
12/31/Year 1 #5 - Bob sells a water heater.		$450.00			$2,465.00
12/31/Year 1 #5 - Bob sells a water heater.			$15.00		$2,450.00
12/31/Year 1 #6 - Bob fills out his time sheet.			$225.00		$2,225.00
12/31/Year 1 #7 - Bob accounts for overhead exp.			$150.00		$2,075.00
	Total:	$5,600.00	$3,525.00	$2,075.00	$2,075.00
1-1800 Inventory			Beginning Balance:	$0.00	
12/31/Year 1 #3 - Bob goes shopping.		$3,000.00			$3,000.00
12/31/Year 1 #4 - Bob sells a hosebib.			$95.00		$2,905.00
12/31/Year 1 #5 - Bob sells a water heater			$160.00		$2,745.00
	Total:	$3,000.00	$255.00	$2,745.00	$2,745.00
1-2100 Truck - Original Cost			Beginning Balance:	$0.00	
12/31/Year 1 #2 - Bob buys a truck.		$15,000.00			$15,000.00
	Total:	$15,000.00	$0.00	$15,000.00	$15,000.00
2-2100 Note Payable - Truck Loan			Beginning Balance:	$0.00	
12/31/Year 1 #2 - Bob buys a truck.			$15,000.00		$15,000.00 cr
	Total:	$0.00	$15,000.00	$15,000.00 cr	$15,000.00 cr
3-1000 Paid-in Capital			Beginning Balance:	$0.00	
12/31/Year 1 #1 - Bob takes money from			$5,000.00		$5,000.00 cr
	Total:	$0.00	$5,000.00	$5,000.00 cr	$5,000.00 cr
4-1000 Sales			Beginning Balance:	$0.00	
12/31/Year 1 #4 - Bob sells a hosebib.			$150.00		$150.00 cr
12/31/Year 1 #5 - Bob sells a water heater.			$450.00		$600.00 cr
	Total:	$0.00	$600.00	$600.00 cr	$600.00 cr
5-1000 Materials			Beginning Balance:	$0.00	
12/31/Year 1 #4 - Bob sells a hosebib.		$95.00			$95.00
12/31/Year 1 #5 - Bob sells a water heater.		$160.00			$255.00
	Total:	$255.00	$0.00	$255.00	$255.00
5-2000 Billable Labor			Beginning Balance:	$0.00	
12/31/Year 1 #5 - Bob sells a water heater.		$135.00			$135.00
	Total:	$135.00	$0.00	$135.00	$135.00

continued on next page

EAGLE PLUMBING COMPANY
GENERAL LEDGER
DETAIL TRIAL BALANCE
12/31/YEAR 1 (CONT'D)

5-3000 Permits		Beginning Balance:	$0.00	
12/31/Year 1 #5 - Bob sells a water heater.	$15.00			$15.00
Total:	$15.00	$0.00	$15.00	$15.00
6-1000 Owner's Salary		Beginning Balance:	$0.00	
12/31/Year 1 #6 - Bob fills out timesheet.	$225.00			$225.00
Total:	$225.00	$0.00	$225.00	$225.00
6-2000 Advertising		Beginning Balance:	$0.00	
12/31/Year 1 #7 - Overhead expenses.	$35.00			$35.00
Total:	$35.00	$0.00	$35.00	$35.00
6-3000 Education		Beginning Balance:	$0.00	
12/31/Year 1 #7 - Overhead expenses.	$5.00			$5.00
Total:	$5.00	$0.00	$5.00	$5.00
6-3050 Insurance		Beginning Balance:	$0.00	
12/31/Year 1 #7 - Overhead expenses.	$10.00			$10.00
Total:	$10.00	$0.00	$10.00	$10.00
6-4000 Office Supplies		Beginning Balance:	$0.00	
12/31/Year 1 #7 - Overhead expenses.	$10.00			$10.00
Total:	$10.00	$0.00	$10.00	$10.00
6-4050 Professional Services		Beginning Balance:	$0.00	
12/31/Year 1 #7 - Overhead expenses.	$25.00			$25.00
Total:	$25.00	$0.00	$25.00	$25.00
6-5000 Tools		Beginning Balance:	$0.00	
12/31/Year 1 #7 - Overhead expenses.	$15.00			$15.00
Total:	$15.00	$0.00	$15.00	$15.00
6-5050 Truck Maintenance & Repair		Beginning Balance:	$0.00	
12/31/Year 1 #7 - Overhead expenses.	$30.00			$30.00
Total:	$30.00	$0.00	$30.00	$30.00
6-6000 Uniforms		Beginning Balance:	$0.00	
12/31/Year 1 #7 - Overhead expenses.	$20.00			$20.00
Total:	$20.00	$0.00	$20.00	$20.00
Grand Total:	$24,380.00	$24,380.00		

ANALYZING THE INCOME STATEMENT

Remember, just to make it easy, Bob Bird's first and only day of business in Year 1is December 31st. This is make-believe! So, let's evaluate his Financials. Note that we've added a percentage column to the Income Statement. This is handy! It will make it easier to compare financial reports from different time periods. The numbers will jump around a lot. Trends are easier to spot when you look at the percentages. What information about Eagle Plumbing can be gathered from looking at the Income Statement? What does the Income Statement tell us? (By the way, what would Bob's accountant say at this point? *"Good news, Bob! You won't have to pay Income Tax!"* Of course, that's because he didn't make any money!)

What can Bob do with the information at this point? HINT: Bob has 3 Billable Hours. Analyze the Income Statement in light of that data:

_____

_____

_____

_____

What is Bob's Billable Hour Efficiency? Answer: 3 hours/8 hours = 38%

How does Billable Hour Efficiency impact your Financial Statements?

There is a widely accepted misunderstanding about small shop operators that I will do my best to clear up: "I run a small shop so my overhead is low. That's why I can charge a low price." THIS IS SHEER NONSENSE!

In terms of *total dollars* spent on overhead items, a small shop will spend less than a large shop. BUT, a small shop has fewer Billable hours. Non-Billable hours and other Overhead expenses must be loaded on the Billable hours and passed on to the customer. Bob has only three billable hours and he must "sell" them for enough money to pay all his bills and make a profit. A larger shop spends more dollars on Indirect Expenses, but they can spread those dollars over many more Billable Hours.

It is common for a small shop to have higher costs per Billable Hour than a large shop. With all the things Bob Bird must do as an owner — answer the phone, run for parts, clean up — three billable hours a day may be realistic.

You need to create a Selling Price that covers all your costs of doing business and is based on a realistic number of Billable Hours.

This is it. This is the key to making all the money you want in your business. This is how to make it fun to go to work. **Your Selling Price needs to be based on your costs of doing business applied to a reasonable number of Billable Hours.** *Then* you will have a fighting chance at making your entrepreneurial dreams come true.

SIMPLE BREAK EVEN FORMULA:

The Break Even point is when you don't make any profit but you just cover all costs. Nice number to know! To determine your Break Even cost (excluding materials) per hour...

add up ...   Direct Costs + Indirect Costs   =   Total Costs to Recover

then ...

        Total Costs to recover / Total Hours Billed*   =   Break–Even Cost per Billed Hour

* Or if you sell only products use Total Hours Available to Sell in place of Total Hours Billed.

Back to analyzing Bob Bird's Financials. In summary, Bob could...

- ▲ Create a selling price that is not just pulled out of thin air.
- ▲ Develop a budget with an eye to actual costs.
- ▲ Set sales goals.
- ▲ *Realize he still has a lot to learn about the scorecard...*but he is GETTING SMARTER!

See how the scorecard leads you to management decisions based on fact, not fiction? See how sane this is? Can you imagine that Bob can hardly wait to look at next month's score and see how he did?

Do you see that, because Bob still has Cash, he might not realize that he's in trouble????

BOB BOUNCES BACK!!

"I've had it with this stinking business," Bob whines. "No way to make a decent living." Bob invited Joey to join him for a going-out-of-business drink.

"Bob," his friend Joey says sharply, "The problem is YOU."

"What do you mean? I did my best! Lost $180 in one day of business. It's the economy!" Bob is grasping at any excuse.

Joey is an accomplished businessman. Made a fortune with a computer repair service called "The Revenge of the Geeks". He shakes his head and says, "Bob, you just need to look at the scorecard of your business. You kept track of everything! That was great! Go back to the Income Statement, figure out your costs and sell your services for more than it costs you to provide them. Quit your whining and get to work!"

The pilot light in Bob's soul starts to burn a bit brighter. "Joey, you really think I can pull off running my own company?"

"Of course you can. It's not that hard. Just pay attention to the score, and the game will be fun!"

Bob pays for the drinks and heads back to Eagle Plumbing. This time he will SOAR!!!!

Let's peek into the future and look at a year's worth of data. Assume Bob established a new selling price for labor and has a whole year under his belt. He also hired a plumber to help him. Now, what do we know about Eagle Plumbing Company??

EAGLE PLUMBING COMPANY
PROFIT & LOSS STATEMENT

JANUARY 1, YEAR 2 THROUGH DECEMBER 31, YEAR 2

	Year to Date	% of YTD Sales
Income		
Sales	$300,000.00	100.0%
Total Income	$300,000.00	100.0%
Direct Costs		
Materials	$60,000.00	20.0%
Billable Labor	$57,000.00	19.0%
Permits	$3,000.00	1.0%
Total Direct Costs	$120,000.00	40.0%
Gross Profit	$180,000.00	60.0%
Indirect Costs		
Owner's Salary	$45,000.00	15.0%
Non-Billable Labor	$25,000.00	8.3%
Advertising	$1,875.00	0.6%
Depreciation	$2,650.00	0.9%
Education	$1,015.00	0.3%
Insurance	$1,400.00	0.5%
Interest on Truck Loan	$2,035.00	0.7%
Miscellaneous	$2,500.00	0.8%
Office Supplies	$1,320.00	0.4%
Professional Services	$1,425.00	0.5%
Shop Supplies	$13,400.00	4.5%
Tools	$5,390.00	1.8%
Truck Maintenance & Repair	$6,455.00	2.2%
Uniforms	$1,535.00	0.5%
Total Indirect Costs	$111,000.00	37.0%
Operating Profit	$69,000.00	23.0%
Other Expenses		
Taxes	$9,000.00	3.0%
Total Other Expenses	$9,000.00	3.0%
Net Profit / (Loss)	$60,000.00	20.0%

EAGLE PLUMBING COMPANY
BALANCE SHEET
DECEMBER 31, YEAR 2

Assets
  Current Assets

Cash	$14,725.00		
Accounts Receivable	$45,450.00		
Inventory	$14,795.00		
Total Current Assets		$74,970.00	
Vehicles			
Truck - Original Cost	$15,000.00		
Truck - Accum. Depreciation	($2,650.00)		
Total Vehicles		$12,350.00	
Total Assets			$87,320.00
Liabilities			
Current Liabilities			
Accounts Payable	$10,000.00		
Total Current Liabilities		$10,000.00	
Long Term Liabilities			
Note Payable - Truck Loan	$12,500.00		
Total Long Term Liabilities		$12,500.00	
Total Liabilities			$22,500.00
Equity			
Paid-in Capital		$5,000.00	
Retained Earnings		($180.00)	
Current Year Earnings		$60,000.00	
Total Equity			$64,820.00
Total Liability & Equity			$87,320.00

Analyze Eagle Plumbing's Financial Statement for Year 2.

Make some observations and jot them down:

_____

_____

_____

_____

Bob has come a long way and knows much more about business than he did a year ago! And the best part...HIS COMPANY GENERATED $60,000 IN PROFITS AND $45,000 IN OWNER'S COMPENSATION! GETTING BETTER!

Note: Here are some "extra credit" items…
▲ Check out the Truck under Assets...what happened to it? Depreciation!
▲ Notice the corresponding Depreciation Expense.
▲ Look at the Truck Loan...note the impact loan payments make. Do you see the Interest Expense on the Income Statement?
▲ What is Bob's Current Ratio? Think he is paying his bills on time? It should be AT LEAST 1:1.
▲ Note that there are Accounts Payable and Accounts Receivable — remember these are promises...A/R is the amount promised to Bob by his customers for work done. A/P is the amount Bob has promised to pay his vendors.
▲ What's still missing? Community contributions! Retirement and benefits for Bob and his employee!
▲ Did Bob make less than his employee? Is that OK?

Now, look at your own Financials and evaluate them. Write your observations below:

_____

_____

_____

_____

_____

_____

_____

_____

How Much Should You Make?

It is common for the owner of a small business to make absolutely NO money! They never pay themselves. The owner even justifies it..."I don't need much. I just like the freedom of running my own company." Blah, blah, blah. I think it's a crime when folks don't make any money. In fact, it comes out of my pocket when they don't pay taxes for roads and schools! **You have an obligation to support yourself, your family and your community.**

How much is enough? Well, it should be more than you can make working for someone else doing the same work. You have greater risk and responsibility as a business owner. How much is too much? Frankly, I don't see the high end. Making money doesn't make you a good guy or a bad guy. How you spend your money is a better indicator of your integrity and character. YOU must decide what you want to make and create a selling price that ensures that you get it. Some food for thought...

> UPS drivers make over $50,000 a year when you add up their benefits. Union auto workers average $80,000 to $90,000 including benefits. Pro-basketball players average $2 million per year. Nice benefits. The average small business owner makes about $35,000. No benefits. No vacation pay. No time off.

Remember you can't do wonderful things — contribute to charities, education, fuel someone else's dreams, care for your family — with money that you don't have. Decide what you want to make. Write it down. Put it in your selling price. Make your dreams come true.

Remember, the next book in this business basics series is called *How Much Should I Charge?*

Call me at 1-877-MAXROHR to order. It tells you how to create a selling price that will make sure that you make the money you want!

HERE'S A HANDY CHECKLIST TO HELP YOU ANALYZE YOUR FINANCIAL STATEMENTS:

▲ How does the data enter the accounting system? Is everyone involved in data entry and accounting fully trained? Don't assume accuracy!!

▲ Are your company's Financials complete and ready for your analysis by the 10th of the following month?

▲ Compare the Financials to last month, last year — same month, year to date.

▲ Look at the percentage column. Ratios are ultimately more important than the dollar amounts.

▲ Look for trends, changes that are more visible over the span of a few months.

▲ Notice if an account that generally has a positive balance suddenly has a negative balance…and vice versa.

▲ Look at the actual Financials in comparison to your budget. Are you close?

▲ Track and analyze Billable hours. This information in not found on the Financials directly. You'll have to track them from the invoices and the timesheets. Determine your Break Even per hour for the month.

▲ Talk to your managers about any discrepancies or questions you have about the information. Ask them what is going on with the numbers before you start dictating solutions. Work together.

▲ Share the data with your employees. Don't feel like you have to know everything about accounting. You can learn together and help each other.

▲ Think of creative ways to improve performance.

▲ Set goals or review and revise goals.

▲ Think of better ways to collect data and gather information.

▲ File one copy for safe keeping, plenty of others for handy access.

▲ Stay curious.

▲ Have fun.

> *"Perhaps the most valuable result of all education is the ability to make yourself do the thing you have to do when it ought to be done whether you like it or not; it is the first lesson that ought to be learned; and however early a man's training begins, it is probably the last lesson he learns thoroughly."*
>
> – T.H. HUXLEY

Concise, consistent data is the key! There is no perfect way to keep score.

Just do it…over and over and over.

Extra-Credit, Bonus Round

Now, if you really want to get a handle on your financial situation, you will look at the relationships between the items on the Balance Sheet.

These are called RATIOS

Let me define a couple of ratios for you. Pay attention to them. Over time, ratios can tell you more than the dollar amounts about the financial condition of your business.

CURRENT RATIO: Current Assets to Current Liabilities

This measures your liquid assets (current assets) against the amount of bills you are going to have to pay in the near future (current liabilities). If you have 2:1 current assets to current liabilities, good for you. That means you have two times as much in current assets as you owe in current liabilities. You have a bit of a safety margin and you should be able to pay your bills as they become due. Keep an eye on your current ratio. If it drops to 1:1 you are in real danger of getting behind on your bills.

DEBT TO EQUITY RATIO: Total Liabilities to Total Owner's Equity

This measures how much you *owe* to how much you *own*. Some debt is good...using other people's money to grow your business can be a necessity. Too much debt is dangerous. A ratio of 1:1 would be considered a modest debt to equity ratio. A ratio of 20:1 would be considered *highly leveraged*.

Banks will look at this ratio before they loan you any money. If the bank thinks you have too much debt, it won't loan you any more money. Over time, profitable business operations will increase your equity, shifting the ratio. This will allow you the freedom to borrow more money to expand your business.

Ultimately, the amount of debt that you want to carry is a personal decision. Some folks like to use as much of other people's money as they can get. Others sleep better at night knowing they are debt free.

Try Again.

Do you know more this time around?

1. Another term for Overhead is…
   ( ) Indirect Costs
   ( ) Liabilities
   ( ) Expenses
   ( ) A type of garage door

2. Which of the following items is not found on a Balance Sheet?
   ( ) Inventory
   ( ) Assets
   ( ) Direct Costs
   ( ) Accumulated Depreciation
   ( ) Equity

3. How is the basic accounting formula usually represented?
   ( ) Sales - Direct Costs = Net Profits
   ( ) Assets = Liabilities + Owner's Equity
   ( ) Assets - Expenses = Net Equity
   ( ) All of the above

4. Billable hours refers to …
   ( ) The direct labor hours for which you bill the customer.
   ( ) The time your bookkeeper spends sending invoices to your customers.
   ( ) The total time your technician is available to do service work.
   ( ) The amount of hours for which you paid your techs, minus the hours actually worked.
   ( ) All of the above.
   ( ) None of the above.

5. It is possible to have a net loss for the month and still have enough cash to run the business for the next two months…true or false?

6. It is possible to have 20% net profit for the year to date and not have enough cash to run the business for one more month…true or false?

7. Below is a list of expense items. Circle the ones that are Direct Costs.

Materials	Tools	Training Seminars
Trucks	Office Supplies	Billable Labor Costs
Permits	Sales commission	Owner's Salary

8. Sales - Direct Costs = _____.

9. Another name for Direct Costs is…
   ( ) Expenses
   ( ) Overhead
   ( ) Cost of Goods Sold
   ( ) Job Site Expenses
   ( ) Those that your boss directed you to expense.

10. What is your deadline to close your books each month? Date_____ and when do you receive the financial statements for the previous month? Date_____

11. *Currently,* when you read your company's financial statements, you …
    ( ) look at trends.
    ( ) look at the past month's activity compared to the year to date numbers.
    ( ) look at budgeted vs. actual amounts.
    ( ) compare this year's activity to the same month in past years.
    ( ) all of the above.
    ( ) none of the above.

12. After you have looked at your company's financial statements, you…
    ( ) file them properly.
    ( ) thank your accountant and pay the bill for his services.
    ( ) call in your managers to explain any discrepancies or questions you have about the information.
    ( ) share the financial information with your employees.
    ( ) think of creative ways to improve performance.
    ( ) all of the above.
    ( ) none of the above.

13. A Chart of Accounts is…
    ( ) the way you code accounting information.
    ( ) the labels under which you file your accounting information.
    ( ) the General Ledger and classifications used in accounting.
    ( ) all of the above.

14. Do you know how much money is necessary, on average, to cover Overhead expenses every month?
    ( ) Yes , $_____   ( ) No, help me!

15. The Income Statement…
    ( ) is another name for the Balance Sheet.
    ( ) summarizes sales revenues and expenses over a period of time.
    ( ) lists the assets, liabilities and owner's equity of your company.
    ( ) all of the above.
    ( ) none of the above.

16. Remember the goal you wrote down for yourself today? Did you accomplish it?

> If you need a bit more help on a couple of the questions, refer to the Answer Sheet on the next page!

Answer Sheet

Use this information to...

▲ Clear up any words that may still be a little "foggy."

▲ Help someone else learn what the heck Financial Statements are!

1. Another term for Overhead is…
    (x) Indirect Costs
    ( ) Liabilities
    ( ) Expenses
    ( ) A type of garage door

Go to your own Financial Statements. Find the Income Statement. The expenses below the Gross Margin (a.k.a. Gross Profit) line are the Overhead, a.k.a. Indirect Costs. Also see pages 47-51.

2. Which of the following items is not found on a Balance Sheet?
    ( ) Inventory
    ( ) Assets
    (x) Direct Costs
    ( ) Accumulated Depreciation
    ( ) Equity

Find your Balance Sheet. Do you see Direct Costs (a.k.a. Cost of Goods Sold, Job Site Expenses?) I hope not. Look on the Income Statement. Do you see Direct Costs — Materials, Labor, Permits — listed there as either Direct Costs or Cost of Goods Sold? I hope so! Also see pages 14 and 47-51.

3. How is the basic accounting formula usually represented?
    ( ) Sales - Direct Costs = Net Profits
    (x) Assets = Liabilities + Owner's Equity
    ( ) Assets - Expenses = Net Equity
    ( ) All of the above

Here's a clue...your Balance Sheet is based on this formula. Look at your Balance Sheet. See it? If not, refer to pages 14-15.

4. Billable hours refers to …
    (x) The direct labor hours for which you bill the customer.
    ( ) The time your bookkeeper spends sending invoices to your customers.
    ( ) The total time your technician is available to do service work.
    ( ) The amount of hours for which you paid your techs, minus the hours actually worked.
    ( ) All of the above.
    ( ) None of the above.

You won't find this information directly on the Financial Statements! You need to keep track from Timesheets and Invoices. Ideally the hours that you bill the customer (Billable Hours) match the hours that the tech spends on the job for the customer. See page 52.

5.   It is possible to have a net loss for the month and still have enough cash to run the business for the next two months? True.

You know what using your credit card can do to you, right? Also, see pages 33-34.

6.   It is possible to have 20% net profit for the year to date and not have enough cash to run the business for one more month? True.

Look at your Income Statement. See the Accounts Receivable line? You can have lots of Sales but little Cash to show for it. Also, see pages 33-34.

7.   Below is a list of expense items. Circle the ones that are Direct Costs.
      Materials
                                   Billable Labor Costs
      Permits   Sales commission

You can make a case for Tools if you totally use up the life of a tool on a particular job. The idea is that Direct Costs are those expenses directly created on the job (Job Site Expenses). Look to your Income Statement and see if you list the circled items under Sales but before Gross Margin. Also, see pages 47-51.

8.   Sales - Direct Costs = <u>Gross Margin</u>.

Refer to your Income Statement. It can also be called Gross Profit. See pages 50-51.

9.   Another name for Direct Costs is...
      ( ) Expenses
      ( ) Overhead
      (x) Cost of Goods Sold
      (x) Job Site Expenses
      ( ) Those that your boss directed you to expense.

One reason why Accounting can be confusing is that there are often several names for the same thing! Look up Direct Cost in the Glossary. What name is used on your Income Statement?

10.   What is your deadline to close your books each month? Date_____ and when do you receive the financial statements for the previous month? Date_____

Could you close the books by the 5th of the next month and have Final Financial Statements by the 10th? Could you do mid-month reports to see if you are on track? Could you run Financial reports every week? Sure, you could!

11.   *Currently,* when you read your company's financial statements, you ...
      ( ) look at trends.
      ( ) look at the past month's activity compared to the year to date numbers.
      ( ) look at budgeted vs. actual amounts.
      ( ) compare this year's activity to the same month in past years.

(x) all of the above.
( ) none of the above.

See page 74 for a checklist to get you started.

12. After you have looked at your company's financial statements, you…
( ) file them properly.
( ) thank your accountant and pay the bill for his services.
( ) call in your managers to explain any discrepancies or questions you have about the information.
( ) share the financial information with your employees.
( ) think of creative ways to improve performance.
(x) all of the above.
( ) none of the above.

One reason that I am a proponent of Open Book Management is that your employees can HELP you analyze the Financial Statements. You can learn this stuff together. See the handy checklist on page 74..

13. A Chart of Accounts is…
( ) the way you code accounting information.
( ) the labels under which you file your accounting information.
( ) the General Ledger and classifications used in accounting.
(x) all of the above.

The Chart of Accounts is the "Peg Board" on which the whole Accounting-Information system hangs. See page 18. Do you have a copy of your Chart of Accounts? Print one up. Look for the patterns in the numbering system. See the big picture! BE WARNED, however. Don't change the Chart of Accounts without the help and support of your accountant and computer system expert!!! Doesn't mean you shouldn't change it, just be careful not to mess up the information system in the process — a real possibility if you're not an expert in accounting or computerized accounting systems.

14. Do you know how much money is necessary, on average, to cover Overhead expenses every month?
( ) Yes , $_____   ( ) No, help me! Call me toll-free at 1-877-MAXROHR.

Do you see the Overhead (a.k.a. Indirect Costs, Operating Expenses) section of the Income Statement? Now seek out past months' and past years' Income Statements. Do some averaging. Can you see the dollar amount that you need to cover Overhead expenses each month come into focus? Can you see how you can budget in future expenses or increases in expenses? Cool, huh?

15. The Income Statement…
( ) is another name for the Balance Sheet.
(x) summarizes sales revenues and expenses over a period of time.
( ) lists the assets, liabilities and owner's equity of your company.
( ) all of the above.
( ) none of the above.

The Income Statement is a magnifying-glass look at the changes in Equity in the company during a period of time. Simply, $$$ in, $$$ out...what's left? See pages 35-36.

Closing Thoughts....

WHERE DID THE MONEY GO??

So now you know that the money goes to pay *all* the costs of doing business. And even in the smallest home-based companies most of the money goes to the *indirect costs* of doing business: the little bills that filter in while you are busy doing the selling and servicing.

Not enough money goes to YOU, the owner. You have all the risk and headache and yet you are usually the last person paid. Sometimes you don't get paid at all.

Traditional business advice is "If you aren't making enough money, cut your overhead." Really? Could you offer the power company less than the total amount due on your utility bill? The only person who would take less if you choose to cut overhead is YOU. That doesn't seem fair to me.

My friend, **I suggest that your overhead is not large enough!** Owner's salary is an overhead item. So are benefits for you and your employees. Your salary and benefits are probably way too low...that's why you picked this book up in the first place.

Use this book to discover and use financial statements. They are the scorecard of your business. By merely *paying attention* to the score, your score will improve.

> *"That which you recognize, you energize."*
> – MARK VICTOR HANSEN

Please understand that I don't suggest that you run an undisciplined, wasteful company, with overhead needlessly inflated. But, my experience tells me that most small business owners are woefully underestimating the realistic costs involved with running a business. Certainly seek to run at maximum efficiency. Just don't fry up yourself and your team in the process by taking too little from your customers to make it worth your while.

I wish you courage and strength and tenacity. You will need these things when you realize you need to raise your prices. I suspect that that is what you will find once you get familiar with your company's scorecard — the financial statements.

If you are going to charge more, then you are going to have to give more. More service, love, attention, good manners, and value. Customers will gladly pay you for those things.

You will do your customers a great disservice if you go out of business. Most businesses DON'T make it — 85% crash within the first 5 years. I just don't believe it is because the owners are lazy. Every business owner I know is going full speed and working well over 40 hours a week. They fail to keep track of the business, they don't keep score. That's why they fail. **If you keep score you can identify your problems...and fix them.**

This book will help you make sense of your scorecard. Business can be a fun game, where all players can win: owner, employees, customers, suppliers, the community...the universe!

One more thing...

OPEN BOOK MANAGEMENT

Consider operating as an open book company. Here's an article from *Plumbing & Mechanical* magazine. I wrote about Jack Stack...a guru in "open book" management.

Want to Play the Game?

"How do you get your technicians to buy in? When we made the switch to Flat Rate pricing, they all assumed the increase in our selling price went straight to my pocket!"

Sound familiar? I hear this question at least once a day! I suggest, if you want your employees to really buy in to your prices, show them where the money goes. Open your books. Teach them how the business works.

My wise suggestion is often rejected.

"If they knew how bad the numbers were, they would all leave!"

"Frankly, I don't know how to read the financial statements myself!"

"It's none of their business how much money I make!"

Do it anyway. If your financial situation is bad, your employees know something is wrong. Their speculation will be much worse than knowing the truth. If you are not comfortable with financial data, you all can learn together. If you don't want to lay open your paycheck, you can ease into open book management by sharing some financial data now, and granting more access later.

Make a game of it!

Recently, I had the pleasure of meeting some folks who play the game very well! I attended a terrific seminar at the Springfield Remanufacturing Company (SRC) in Springfield, Missouri.

The Great Game of Business!

Jack Stack is CEO of SRC. SRC rebuilds engines. (They don't do plumbing, but, no matter. Read on.) Jack previously worked at International Harvester as a mid-level manager. At the time, International Harvester was $6 billion in debt with interest rates at 20% and they were laying off 1,000 workers a day. (You think you've got problems.)

Jack decided that there must be a saner way to run a business than the my-way-or-highway management philosophy that was sinking International Harvester. Faced with laying off the remaining 119 employees, Jack and a dozen other managers came up with a plan to buy their division of the company.

Jack didn't really know much about business at the time. As they went from bank to bank seeking a loan (21 total!), he learned how to interpret the financial statements. Their numbers were horrible. By some error, I imagine, the 21st bank loaned the company $89 million with collateral of $100,000.00, borrowed from friends and relatives. Springfield Remanufacturing Company was in business!

Because of their fragile financial position, the company couldn't afford to be late on one payment or they would lose the company. Jack had no idea how he was going to pull it off. So, he turned to the employees and said, "We need to generate enough cash and profits to stay afloat. I don't know how to do it. Here are the financial statements. This is how we keep track of what's going on. I need your help!"

Every employee learned the financial side of the business. They made the connection that what they did at each work station impacted some number on the income statement or balance sheet. The employees saved the day! They took responsibility for the turnaround of the plant and pulled it off.

As the employees learned the game of business, they became eager to play bigger, more interesting games. Today SRC is comprised of 23 diversified companies, one of which produces the terrific seminar I attended explaining their take on open book management. The focus is not on manufacturing…it is about doing business in an open, cooperative, creative, *responsible* way.

The success of SRC makes a great story. So Jack Stack wrote a book, *The Great Game of Business*. It outlines the system that evolved at SRC. It is not an instant or exact formula. At the Great Game Seminar, several SRC managers explained the basic components:

1. Know and Teach the Rules.

The rules are dictated by the capital market. In other words, keep track of the money! Oh, I know some of you think there are more important things than money. There are. But we are just talking about the game of business. To play the game, you need to find out how to get money into the company and decide what to do with it when it gets there.

The Balance Sheet and the Income Statement are the principle scorecards. Don't feel bad if you don't really understand these reports. Jack claims a huge majority of the business population is financially illiterate. (Frank Blau says that more than 90% of the people who attend his seminars can't correctly compute a selling price!) But you can learn and share your knowledge with your employees as you go. At SRC, 30% of every new employee's time is spent learning the financial aspect of the business. Everybody plays the game.

By creating, analyzing and communicating the financial statements, you can find the numbers that really indicate the condition of the company. By setting targets for these "critical numbers" you lay out the rules of the game. (In your company consider starting with the Gross Margin.)

Do you see that if your employees have a stake in the process of determining the "critical numbers" and setting the goals, they commit themselves to winning the game? Are you getting a glimpse of how cool this can be??

2. Follow the Action and Keep Score.

Hold regular meetings to go over all the numbers. How are you doing with actual sales versus predicted sales? Are you over-budget on advertising because you couldn't resist the salesman with the talking refrigerator magnets? The numbers make everyone accountable! I love this! Especially refreshing in our point-the-finger society.

At SRC, there is a person responsible for every line on the financial statements. The numbers aren't cold, nasty, unrelated facts. One number may indicate that Suzy in Accounts Receivable is struggling with collections. The group can offer suggestions: improve C.O.D. procedures, quit selling to deadbeats, etc.

I used to think it was cool to get financial data within ten days of the next month. SRC employees report mid-month figures. They can nip a problem before the month ends!

The financial statements provide the agenda for the meeting. As you go through each item on the Income Statement and Balance Sheet, you check in with each department, see what's happening and decide on a course of action.

3. Provide a Stake in the Outcome.

You must be able to win the game and reap the rewards. If the only one who wins is you, the team won't carry you for long. Poll your employees to find out what they value...money, time off, education, insurance benefits. Create a bonus system and tie the bonus to hitting the critical numbers.

It's important to have a company-wide critical number goal. But be careful to reward individual performance as well. Often one outstanding employee is pulling the whole company along while the boss boasts about teamwork! People who contribute more should get more. Every position in the company can be tied to an incentive-based compensation plan.

SRC has a Employee Stock Ownership Plan (ESOP). This is a very hip way to tie compensation to the company's performance. Dish out stock to the owner-employees as a bonus for hitting the marks. Stock bonuses don't require immediate cash disbursement. But they are only worth something if the company improves in value by creating solid earnings! This is the ultimate buy-in.

4. You Gotta Wanna!

"You Gotta Wanna"...Jack calls this one of the Higher Laws of Business. Motivation comes from within. Your techs will be comfortable selling their services at a reasonable price when they believe in the price. If they understand every cost associated with developing the price, they can sell it. If they see how the customer benefits from the unique way that you do business and understand the costs associated with customer service, they can sell it. If they see what's in it for them, they will want to sell it. They gotta wanna.

As you play the game, your techs and the rest of the team will *help* you develop the selling price, using their keen knowledge of your company's financial data. They may even suggest a raise for you!

Your employees can win the game and make your company successful. You don't have to do it all by yourself. How wonderful to share in the success. Jack says, the *Ultimate Higher Law in Business* is… "When you appeal to the highest level of thinking, you get the highest level of performance." Good stuff!

Some parting words…

▲ It takes time and relentless training to really play the game.

▲ The process builds trust…in the process! And in each other.

▲ Visit the Great Game website (www.greatgame.com) for more information.

▲ Buy and read the book *The Great Game of Business* by Jack Stack.

Remember Monopoly? You love playing it. But, it's no fun all by yourself. Invite everyone to play and create a wonderful game with your business.

First printed in *Plumbing & Mechanical* magazine July 1997.

GLOSSARY

ACCOUNTING EQUATION: The Balance Sheet is based on the basic accounting equation. That is:

Assets = Equities

Equity of the company can be held by someone other than the owner. That is called a liability. Because we always have some liabilities, the accounting equation is usually written...

Assets = Liabilities + Owner's Equity

ACCOUNTS: Business activities cause increases and decreases in your assets, liabilities and equity. Your accounting system records these activities in *accounts*. A number of accounts are needed to summarize the increases and decreases in each asset, liability and owner's equity account on the Balance Sheet and of each revenue and expense that appears on the Income Statement. You can have a few accounts or hundreds, depending on the kind of detailed information you need to run your business.

ACCOUNTS PAYABLE: Also called A/P. These are bills that your business owes to the government or your suppliers. If you have bought it, but haven't paid for it yet (like when you buy on account), you create an account payable. These are found in the liability section of the Balance Sheet.

ACCOUNTS RECEIVABLE: Also called A/R. When you sell something to someone, and they don't pay you that minute, you create an account receivable. This is the amount of money your customers owe you for products and services that they bought from you but haven't paid for yet. Accounts receivable are found in the current assets section of the Balance Sheet.

ACCRUAL BASIS ACCOUNTING: With accrual basis accounting, you "account for" expenses and sales at the time the transaction occurs. This is the most accurate way of accounting for your business activities. If you sell something to Mrs. Fernwicky today, you would record the sale as of today, even if she plans on paying you in two months. If you buy some paint today, you account for it today, even if you will pay for it next month when the supply house statement comes.

ASSETS: The 'stuff' the company owns. Anything of value - cash, accounts receivable, trucks, inventory, land. **Current assets** are those that could be converted into cash easily (officially, within a year's time). The most current of current assets is cash, of course. Accounts receivable will be converted to cash as soon as the customer pays, hopefully within a month. So, accounts receivable are current assets. So is inventory.

Fixed assets are those things that you wouldn't want to convert into cash for operating money. For instance, you don't want to sell your building to cover the supply house bill. Assets are listed in order of *liquidity* (how close it is to cash) on the Balance Sheet.

BALANCE SHEET: The Balance Sheet reflects the financial condition of the company on a specific date. The basic accounting formula is the basis for the Balance Sheet:

Assets = Liabilities + Owner's Equity

The Balance Sheet doesn't start over. It is the cumulative score from day one of the business to the time the report is created.

BILLABLE HOUR: The labor hour that is sold as a service to the customer. For instance, a doctor's exam requires the doctor's time. If your service involves your time, the billable hour is a very important number. There are only 24 hours in a day and you and your employees can be of service for only so many of those hours every day. How many? You must keep track with timecards...tallied daily, weekly, monthly, and yearly.

Doctors, plumbers, painters, house cleaners, lawyers, baby-sitters...are all limited by the number of hours that they have to provide their services. Knowing your billable hours can help make sure that you are charging enough for your services. All the costs of doing business must be recaptured by the sale of your billable hours.

Some activities in your business can not be directly billed to a customer — like sweeping the shop. These are called non-billable hours. The costs for these hours must be included in the selling price of the billable hours. (Learn how to price your services — call 1.877.629.7647 toll free and order *How Much Should I Charge?*, a beginner's guide to setting a selling price.)

The ratio of billable hours to the total hours available is called **billable hour efficiency**.

CASH BASIS ACCOUNTING: records the sale when the cash is received and the expense when the check goes out. Not as accurate a picture of what is happening at your company.

CASH FLOW: The movement and timing of money in and out of the business. In addition to the Balance Sheet and the Income Statement, you may want to report the flow of cash through your business. Your company could be profitable but 'cash poor' and unable to pay your bills. Not good!

A **cash flow statement** helps keep you aware of how much cash came and went for any period of time. A **cash flow projection** would be an educated guess at what the cash flow situation will be for the future — you could use this for your budget.

Suppose you want to buy a new truck with cash. But that purchase will empty the bank account and leave you without any cash for payroll! For cash flow reasons, you might choose to buy a truck on payments instead.

CHART OF ACCOUNTS: A complete listing of every account in your accounting system. Every transaction in your business needs to be recorded so that you can keep track of things. Think of the chart of accounts as the peg board on which you hang the business activities.

CREDIT: A credit is used in Double-Entry accounting to increase a liability or an equity account. A credit will decrease an asset account. For every credit there is a debit. These are the two balancing components of every journal entry. Credits and debits keep the basic accounting equation (Assets = Liabilities + Owner's Equity) in balance as you record business activities.

DEBIT: A debit is used in Double-Entry accounting to increase an asset account. A debit will decrease a liability or an equity account. For every debit there is a credit. Note the handy debit and credit rules chart at the end of the book.

DEPRECIATION and **ACCUMULATED DEPRECIATION:** Depreciation means expensing an asset over a period of time. Depreciation is recorded as an expense and shows up on the Income Statement. The balancing Double-Entry is recorded in accumulated depreciation, an account that shows the total amount of depreciation you have recorded for an asset. Accumulated depreciation appears on the Balance Sheet, right below the asset.

For example, let's say you have a truck that you use for deliveries. Tax laws allow you to expense the cost of that truck over the course of a few years. Each month you will make a journal entry that records the depreciation.

	Debit	Credit
Depreciation Expense	$700	
Accumulated Depreciation		$700

And the truck would be listed on the Balance Sheet like this…

Assets		
Truck		$20,000
Accumulated Depreciation	($700)	

So the asset is listed at its original cost and the accumulated depreciation account right below it tells you how much of the total cost of the asset has been expensed. You see, that asset will reduce in value over time, right? The asset less the accumulated depreciation amount gives you a rough estimate of the value of the vehicle.

This is an accounting technique. It isn't intended to show you the actual re-sale value of the truck! Some assets increase in value over time. Some lose their value or get 'used up' (like a truck). Depreciation allows you to expense an asset that gets used up over time.

Note that depreciation is a non-cash expense. You don't get a bill in the mail every month saying, "Pay your depreciation!" The idea is that you *could* take the dollar amount that you are depreciating every month and put it in the bank. When five years are up (typically, you depreciate a truck over five years) you take that money and buy the company a new truck!

Now, consider this…could you replace the truck you have today with one of equal value in five years for the same selling price? In other words, if you bought a brand new truck in 1998 for $25,0000, would you expect the new 2003 model trucks to sell for $25,000? By then, a similar truck might cost $40,000. Depreciation can help you plan for replacing your truck but it is not the whole story. (The next book in this business basics series is called *How Much Should I Charge?* It helps you create a selling price that will make sure you can afford a new truck when you need one. Reach me at 1.877.629.7647 — and order a copy.)

Depreciation is a handy method for expensing an asset that loses value when you use it in your business. Office Furniture is another asset that gets used up, so you are allowed by tax law to depreciate it.

DIRECT COSTS: Also called cost of goods sold, cost of sales or job site expenses. These are expenses that include labor costs and materials. These expenses can be directly tracked to a specific job. If the job didn't happen, the direct costs wouldn't have been incurred. (Compare direct cost with indirect costs to get a better understanding of the term.) Direct costs are found on the Income Statement, right below the income accounts.

Income - Direct Costs = Gross Margin

DOUBLE-ENTRY ACCOUNTING: An accounting system used to keep track of business activities. Double-Entry accounting maintains the Balance Sheet:

Assets = Liabilities + Owner's Equity

When dollars are recorded in one account, they must be accounted for in another account in such a way that the activity is well documented and the Balance Sheet stays in balance.

You may not need to be an expert in Double-Entry accounting, but the person who is responsible for creating the financial statements better get pretty good at it. If that is you, go back through the book and focus on the 'gray' sheets. Study the examples and see how the Double-Entry method acts as a check and balance of your books.

Remember the law of the universe…what goes around, comes around. This is the essence of Double-Entry accounting.

EQUITY: Funds that have been supplied to the company to get the "stuff." Equities show ownership of the assets or claims against the assets. If someone other than the owner has claims on the assets, it is called a **liability.**

Total Assets - Total Liabilities = Net Equity

This is another way of stating the basic accounting equation that emphasizes how much of the assets you own. Net equity is also called **net worth.**

EXPENSE: Also called costs. Expenses are decreases in equity. These are dollars paid out to suppliers, vendors, Uncle Sam, employees, charities, etc. Remember to pay bills thankfully, because it takes money to make money. Expenses are listed on the Income Statement. They should be split into two categories, direct costs and indirect costs. The basic equation for the Income Statement is:

Revenues - Expenses = Profit

(You'll see a profit if there are more revenues than expenses!…or a loss, if expenses are more than revenues.)

Remember, all costs need to be included in your selling price. The customer pays for everything. In exchange, you give the customer your services. What a deal!

FINANCIAL STATEMENTS: refer to the Balance Sheet and the Income Statement. The Balance Sheet is a report that shows the financial condition of the company. The Income Statement (also called the Profit and Loss statement or the P&L) is the profit performance summary.

Financial Statements can include the supporting documents like cash flow reports, accounts receivable reports, transaction register, etc. Any report that measures the movement of money in your company.

Financial Statements are what the bank wants to see before it loans you money. The IRS insists that you share the score with them, and asks for your Financial Statements every year.

GENERAL LEDGER: Once upon a time, accounting systems were kept in a book that listed the increases and decreases in all the accounts of the company. That book was called the general ledger. Today, you probably have a computerized accounting system. Still, the general ledger is a collection of all Balance Sheet and Income Statement accounts...all the assets, liabilities and equity. It is the report that shows ALL the activity in the company. Often this listing is called a detail trial balance on the report menu of your accounting program.

GROSS MARGIN: Also called **gross profit.** This is how much money you have left after you have subtracted the direct costs from the selling price.

Income - Direct Costs = Gross Margin

This is a good number to scrutinize each month, and to track in terms of percentage to total sales over the course of time. The higher the better with gross margin! You need to have enough money left at this point to pay all your indirect costs and still end up with a profit.

If your gross margin isn't high enough to do that, you need to raise your prices. (More on this in Part Two of the Business Basics Series - *How Much Should I Charge?* Visit www.barebonesbiz.com to order!)

INCOME STATEMENT: also called the Profit and Loss Statement, or P&L, or Statement of Operations. This is a report that shows the changes in the equity of the company as a result of business operations. It lists the income (revenues or sales), subtracts the expenses and shows you the profit or loss. This report covers a period of time and summarizes the money in and the money out.

The Income Statement is like a magnifying glass that shows the detail of activities that cause changes in the equity section of the Balance Sheet.

INDIRECT COST: Also called **overhead or operating expenses**. These expenses are indirectly related to the services you provide to customers. Indirect costs include office salaries, rent, advertising, telephone, utilities...costs to keep a 'roof overhead'. Every cost that is not a direct cost is an indirect cost. Indirect costs *do not* go away when sales drop off.

INVENTORY: Also called **stock.** These are materials that you purchase with the intent to sell, but you haven't sold them yet. Inventory is found on the balance sheet under assets. It is considered a current asset because you will convert it into cash as soon as you sell it.

JOURNAL: This is the diary of your business. It keeps track of business activities chronologically. Each business activity is recorded as a journal entry. The Double-Entry will list the debit account and the credit account for each transaction on the day that it occurred. In your reports menu in your accounting system, the journal entries are listed in the **transaction register.**

LIABILITIES: Like equities, these are sources of assets — how you got the "stuff." These are claims against assets by someone other than the owner. This is what the company owes! Notes payable, taxes payable and loans are liabilities. Liabilities are categorized as **current liabilities** (need to pay off within a year's time, like payroll taxes) or **long term liabilities** (payback time is more than a year, like your building mortgage).

LIQUIDITY: How close it is to cash on the Balance Sheet.

MONEY: Also called moola, scratch, gold, coins, cash, change, chicken feed, jing, green stuff, etc. Money is the form we use to exchange energy, goods and services for other energy, goods and services. Used to buy things that you need or want. Beats trading for chickens in the global marketplace.

Money in and of itself is neither good or bad. I want you to make lots of it, and do *great* things with it!

NET INCOME: Also called **net profit, net earnings, current earnings or bottom line**. (No wonder accounting is confusing — look at all those words that mean the same thing!)

After you have subtracted ALL expenses (including taxes) from revenues, you are left with net income. The word net means basic, fundamental. This is a very important item on the income statement because it tells you how much money is left after business operations. Think of net income like the score of a single basketball game in a series. Net income tells you if you won or lost, and by how much, for a given period of time.

By the way, if net income is a negative number, it's called a loss. You want to avoid those. The net income is reflected on the Balance Sheet in the equity section, under current earnings (or net profit). Net income results in an increase in owner's equity. A loss results in a decrease in owner's equity.

PAID-IN CAPITAL: Money that has been invested in the company by the owner. This is an equity investment.

RETAINED EARNINGS: The amount of net income earned and retained by the business. If net income is like the score after a single basketball game, retained earnings is the lifetime statistic. Retained earnings is found in the equity section of the Balance Sheet. It keeps track of how much of the total owner's equity was earned and retained by the business versus how much capital has been invested from the owners (**paid-in capital**).

Each month, the net profits are reflected in the Balance Sheet as current earnings. At the end of the year, current earnings are added to the retained earnings account.

Summary of Debit and Credit Rules for Maintaining the General Ledger

The six rules for debt and credit are:

▲ To *increase* an asset account, *debit* it.

▲ To *decrease* an asset account, *credit* it.

▲ To *increase* a liability or equity account, *credit* it.

▲ To *decrease* a liability or equity account, *debit* it.

▲ To *record revenues, credit* a revenue account.

▲ To *record expenses, debit* an expense account.

This diagram may help you remember the six rules for debit and credit.

BALANCE SHEET ACCOUNTS

Assets (Example: Cash)		=	**Liabilities** (Example: Accounts Payable)		+	**Equity** (Example: Paid-in Capital)	
Debit	**Credit**		**Debit**	**Credit**		**Debit**	**Credit**
Increase	Decrease		Decrease	Increase		Decrease	Increase
+	–		+	–		+	–

INCOME STATEMENT ACCOUNTS

The Income Statement summarizes the changes in Equity that occur as a result of business operations.

Revenues (Example: Sales		**Expenses** (Example: Owner's Salary)	
Debit	**Credit**	**Debit**	Credit
	Increase	Increase	
	+	+	

Congratulations! You're on your way to making more money!

My mission is to help people make a living doing what they love!

You may think that other folks know the secrets to making money in business. My friend, you can do it! Business is not that hard!! You just need to keep score to be able to play the game well, to know whether or not you're winning, to understand where you need to make adjustments. The key is in your financial statements.

This book is NOT the ultimate small business resource. It is the beginner's guide to basic business scorekeeping. It will teach you how to find out where the money goes. Because it always goes somewhere!

There are a lot of great business books out there. This is the primer, the kindergarten course ... the stuff that is not taught in school or in other books. It assumes you know nothing about business.

Eighty percent of all businesses are either out of business or losing money after a few years of the owner's blood, sweat and tears. My own experiences with my home-based business were awful . . . until I learned the basics. I was fortunate enough to find a mentor — generous with his time and wisdom. (Thanks, Frank Blau!) I would be honored to act as your mentor.

*Reach me at 1-877-629-7647 or via fax at 417-753-3685.
Or e-mail me at ellen@barebonesbiz.com*

*Be sure to visit our website www.barebonesbiz.com
for bare bones business basics. You'll find lots of
tips for making more money and having more fun
in your business.*

*Let me know how you are doing with your business.
I want you to do what you love and make lots of money!*

xoxo — Ellen

Order Information

Use this convenient form to order products from Bare Bones Biz.

Buy these helpful products — 100% NO PROBLEM Money Back Guarantee!

Name: _____

Address: _____

City / State / Zip: _____

Phone: _____

Fax: _____

	Price:	**Quantity:**	**Order:**
"Where Did the Money Go?" by Ellen Rohr	$19.99	_____	_____
"How Much Should I Charge?" by Ellen Rohr	$19.99	_____	_____
Bare Bones Biz Budget Builder...does the math for you!	$29.95	_____	_____

Subtotal = $_____

Shipping
Orders to $50 add $4.00 $_____
Orders over $50 add $8.00 $_____

Subtotal = $_____

MO residents add 5.1% sales tax $_____

TOTAL = $_____

Credit Card (VISA, MC and American Express accepted)

Card Number:_____ Exp. Date:_____

Order via mail, fax or telephone:
www.barebonesbiz.com (THE community for Bare Bones Biz Builders)
3120 S. Know It All Lane
Rogersville, MO 65742
877.629.7647 – toll free
417.753.3685 – fax
ellen@barebonesbiz.com